Rulers of the Material World

Dr. Peter Bonadie

Copyright © 2025 Dr. Peter Bonadie

Printed in the United States of America
ISBN: 979-8-9932128-4-5 for print

All rights reserved solely by the author. The author guarantees all contents are original and do not infringe upon the legal rights of any other person or work. No part of this book may be reproduced, stored in a retrieval system, or transmitted in any form or by any means without expressed written permission of the author.

Scripture quotations taken from the Amplified® Bible (AMP), Copyright © 2015 by The Lockman Foundation. Used by permission. lockman.org

Scripture quotations are from the ESV® Bible (The Holy Bible, English Standard Version®), © 2001 by Crossway, a publishing ministry of Good News Publishers. ESV Text Edition: 2025. The ESV text may not be quoted in any publication made available to the public by a Creative Commons license. The ESV may not be translated in whole or in part into any other language. Used by permission. All rights reserved.

Scripture quotations marked MSG are taken from The Message, copyright © 1993, 2002, 2018 by Eugene H. Peterson. Used by permission of NavPress. All rights reserved. Represented by Tyndale House Publishers.

All quotes, unless otherwise noted, are from the HOLY BIBLE, NEW INTERNATIONAL VERSION (NIV). Copyright © 1973, 1978, 1984 by International Bible Society. Used by permission of Zondervan Publishing House. All rights reserved.

Scripture taken from the New King James Version®. Copyright © 1982 by Thomas Nelson. Used by permission. All rights reserved.

Published by Dr. Peter Bonadie
Kingdom Life Ministries International
770 Park Place
Brooklyn, NY 11210-0264

Editing and Formatting by Lisa Pearson

Dedication
ଔ

I dedicate this work to every believer who has ever dared to dream beyond the boundaries imposed by men, tradition, or fear.

To the visionaries who feel the call of God burning in their bones: the call to rise, to build, to possess, and to rule.

To my spiritual sons and daughters across the nations who understand that the Kingdom is not a theory but a reality to be enforced in every sphere of life.

May you refuse to settle for crumbs when your Father has given you the table. May you walk in the dominion of Christ, unashamedly claiming the earth as your inheritance and shaping history for His glory.

You are the heirs of a borderless Kingdom. Take it.

Acknowledgement

I give all glory and honor to the Lord Jesus Christ, the rightful King of kings, whose Word and Spirit have been the guiding light in the writing of this book. Without His revelation, this work would be nothing more than ink on paper.

I acknowledge my beloved family, who have been my constant source of encouragement and strength. To my wonderful children, Jamima, Crystal, Joshua, and Caleb. You have each, in your own way, inspired me to keep pressing into the deeper things of God and to never compromise the vision He has placed in my heart.

My gratitude also extends to the faithful members and leaders of Kingdom Life Ministries International. Your hunger for truth, your willingness to be stretched, and your boldness to step into uncharted territory have been the living example of the principles taught in these pages.

To my friends, mentors, and fellow laborers in the Gospel who have prayed, advised, and challenged me. You have sharpened my thinking and strengthened my resolve.

And finally, to every reader who will embrace these truths and run with them. You are the reason this book was written. May it ignite in you the courage to believe for the impossible, to claim what Heaven has declared yours, and to walk in the dominion of your God-given inheritance.

Contents

☙

- *i* | Foreword
- *v* | Preface
- 01 | Introduction: Ruling the Seen by Mastering the Unseen
- 05 | Ch. 1: Theological Errors and Painful Inaccuracies of the Church
- 14 | Ch. 2: The Original Intent
- 39 | Ch. 3: The Vast Expanse of the Material World
- 58 | Ch. 4: Patriarchs, Covenants, and Lands
- 69 | Ch. 5: Jesus: Master of the Material World | The King Who Commands Creation
- 82 | Ch. 6: As He Is, So Are We
- 91 | Ch. 7: Historical and Modern Examples of Possessing the Earth by Faith
- 96 | Ch. 8: Promises of Possession: God's Covenant for His People to Inherit the Earth
- 105 | Ch. 9: The War of Worlds: Atrocities for Possession of Land and Wealth

120 | Ch. 10: Territorial Spirits and Why Believers Are Best Positioned to Defeat Them to Own Land Mass

140 | Ch. 11: The Superior Construct of the Human | Unveiling the Divine Design at the Quantum Level

164 | Ch. 12: Strategies for Supernaturally Manipulating the Laws of the Material World

171 | Ch. 13: Territorial Dominion and Generational Wealth Transfer

185 | Ch. 14: Today Is Your Birthday: Ask a Big Gift

206 | Ch. 15: Faith: The Greatest Activator of the Power of God

227 | Appendices

Foreword
ଔ

It is with great honor and joy that I pen this foreword to Dr. Peter Bonadie's groundbreaking work. As I read through these chapters, I felt the weight of a divine summons; one that does not merely inspire, but activates. This is not just another book on theology, wealth, or spiritual warfare. It is a prophetic blueprint for believers who understand that their faith must translate into tangible dominion over the world's resources, systems, and territories.

I have walked with Dr. Bonadie for many years, both as a friend and as a fellow laborer in the Kingdom. I have watched him live the very principles he writes about here. His words are not theoretical musings; they are battle-tested strategies forged in prayer, proven in ministry, and confirmed in real-world engagement with the systems of our time. In an era where many believers settle for surviving within the boundaries the world sets, Dr. Bonadie challenges us to expand those boundaries until they disappear entirely.

This book is both confrontational and empowering. It confronts the spirit of limitation, poverty, and spiritual passivity that has too often crippled the Church. It empowers the reader to see themselves as God sees them: co-heirs with Christ, endowed with the authority to subdue and govern the earth in alignment with Heaven's purposes. From the pages of Scripture to the corridors of history, Dr. Bonadie weaves a compelling case for why God's people must rise as innovators, entrepreneurs, and leaders who set the moral and economic agenda for the nations.

I was particularly struck by his treatment of faith as the master key to possessing nations. The stories of the patriarchs, the insights into territorial spirits, and the call to prophetic strategy all point to one inescapable truth: the believer is meant to be the head and not the tail, above and not beneath (Deuteronomy 28:13). In Dr. Bonadie's hands, this truth becomes more than a familiar verse. It becomes a mandate.

As you turn the pages of this book, I encourage you to do so with an open heart and a ready spirit. This is not a message to admire from a distance; it is a call to action. Your inheritance is not only spiritual, but also practical. Your faith is not only for personal salvation, but for global impact. Your life is not only for survival, but for dominion.

Dr. Bonadie has given us more than a book. He has given us a weapon, a roadmap, and a vision. My prayer is that you will not only read it, but also rise to embody it. The world is waiting, creation is groaning, and the Kingdom is advancing. It's time to take your place.

Apostle Anderson Williams
International Apostle and Thought Leader

Preface
☙

This book was born out of a conviction, a conviction that the people of God have lived far beneath their inheritance for far too long. We have often confined our understanding of faith to personal piety, moral living, and the hope of heaven, while neglecting the clear biblical mandate to subdue the earth, exercise dominion, and govern the material world in alignment with Heaven's blueprint.

As I studied Scripture, a pattern emerged that I could not ignore. From Genesis to Revelation, God's people are not presented as powerless spectators in the unfolding drama of history, but as active participants; shapers of nations, custodians of resources, and influencers of global destiny. Abraham, Joseph, Daniel, and Solomon were not merely spiritual men; they were political, economic, and strategic forces in their time. They navigated kingdoms, influenced rulers, and managed wealth on a scale that impacted generations.

In my travels around the world, I have met believers who love God deeply. However, they live in constant financial, emotional, and territorial defeat because they have not been taught how to connect their spiritual authority to practical dominion. Too often, we have spiritualized away our responsibility to master the systems of the world, leaving those systems in the hands of people who do not share our Kingdom values. This has led to a tragic imbalance: the righteous have the wisdom of God, but the unrighteous possess the levers of power.

This book is my response to that imbalance. It is a call for a holy recalibration; a return to the full scope of what it means to be a son or daughter of God. It is about reclaiming our role as stewards of creation, innovators of culture, and administrators of Heaven's resources on earth. It is about understanding that we are designed to operate not only in the church pew but also in the boardroom, the laboratory, the marketplace, and the corridors of political influence.

Throughout these chapters, you will see that our dominion is not an arrogant grab for control but a sacred trust. We do not claim the earth for personal greed; we claim it for the glory of God and the good of humanity. We stand in the lineage of those who dared to believe God's promises and saw nations bow to the wisdom, creativity, and power of His people. We are heirs of a Kingdom that cannot be shaken and ambassadors of a reign that will have no end.

As you read, my prayer is that your faith will be ignited and your vision expanded. May you see yourself as God sees you: capable of managing resources, shaping policies, innovating technologies, and influencing cultures. May you understand that dominion is not optional for the believer. It is our birthright. And may you step boldly into your assignment, knowing that the same God who called Abraham to walk the length and breadth of the land is calling you to do the same in your generation.

Dr. Peter Bonadie
Brooklyn, New York

Introduction
⚘
Ruling the Seen by Mastering the Unseen

Every civilization has been shaped by those who understood how to harness unseen forces to change the visible world. Ancient kings consulted oracles before going to war. The greatest inventors and innovators were driven by ideas no one could yet see. The most successful entrepreneurs turned invisible concepts into empires of gold. And the most unstoppable believers in Scripture altered history itself by commanding the sun to stand still, parting seas, calling fire from heaven, and multiplying food in famine.

This is not mere poetry, it is a spiritual law. The visible world is governed by the invisible. The tangible is shaped by the intangible. The things you can see, feel, and touch are merely the shadows and echoes of a greater, unseen reality. Hebrews 11:3 declares, *"By faith we understand that the universe was created by the word of God, so that what is seen was not made out of things that are visible."* This is the foundation of all dominion. Until you master the laws of the invisible world, you will always be a servant to those who have.

The great tragedy of the modern church is that many believers live as beggars when God has called them to rule. We pray as if we are powerless. We dream small when God offers kingdoms. We survive when God has commanded us to subdue. Psalm 2:7–8 issues a royal invitation that most believers still ignore: "*The LORD said to me, 'You are my Son; today I have begotten you. Ask of me, and I will make the nations your heritage, and the ends of the earth your possession.'*" God is not offering you a parking spot. He's offering you continents.

The laws that govern the unseen realm are not religious mysteries for a chosen few. They are divine technologies, keys of the Kingdom, placed in the hands of every son and daughter of God. Fasting, decrees, prophetic planning, strategic alliances, skill mastery, and divine creativity are not optional extras. They are tools for governing territories and shaping nations. Jesus did not simply save us from hell. He restored to us the lost mandate of Eden to be fruitful, multiply, replenish the earth, subdue it, and have dominion.

Faith is the activator. It is the master key that unlocks the treasury of Heaven. Faith turns invisible promises into tangible realities. Faith takes the raw materials of thought, declaration, and spiritual law, and forges them into cities, nations, and legacies. This is why Abraham is called the father of faith. Abraham changed the course of history and birthed nations out of nothing but a word from God. His sons and descendants became the wealthiest men of their times, controlling trade routes, resources, and political power. They understood that the covenant was not just spiritual, it was economic, territorial, and generational.

In this book, we will strip away the small thinking that has kept believers trapped in survival mode. You will learn how to command creation, how to activate quantum laws for Kingdom purposes, and how to take your rightful place as an innovator, entrepreneur, pioneer, and thought leader. You will discover how to move from praying safe prayers to making audacious requests that shift history. You will see why billion-dollar ideas are not the property of Silicon Valley alone, but the inheritance of Kingdom citizens who know their God.

This is more than theology. It is strategy for rulership. It is the art and science of taking dominion in the material world by mastering the laws of the invisible one. The greatest entrepreneurs of the future will not merely be those with money, but those who understand Heaven's economy. The next billionaires will not just have patents, they will have prophetic blueprints. The next great innovators will not simply study the market, they will legislate from the throne room of God.

If you are ready to step into the realm where your thoughts and words alter matter, where nations respond to your decrees, and where wealth flows according to covenant promise, then you are ready for the truths in these pages. The time for passive Christianity is over. The time for rulership has come.

Chapter 1

ଔ

Theological Errors and Painful Inaccuracies of the Church

How We Lost the Mandate to Rule the Material World

A Church That Abandoned Half of Its Mandate

When Jesus gave the Great Commission, He did not instruct the Church to withdraw from the world's affairs or to treat material reality as unworthy of attention. He declared, *"All authority in heaven and on earth has been given to me. Therefore go..."* (Matthew 28:18–19).

From Genesis to Revelation, God's mandate for humanity is two-fold: spiritual restoration and material dominion. Yet somewhere in history, the Church, in large part, embraced a theology that magnified spiritual concerns while ignoring material rulership.

The result? We have produced generations of believers who know how to attend prayer meetings but do not know how to manage cities, control industries, or harness resources for Kingdom purposes. We preach about heaven but neglect the earth that God explicitly commanded us to steward. This abandonment of the material-world mandate is not a harmless oversight. It has weakened our witness, diminished our influence, and left much of creation in the hands of those who neither fear God nor honor His ways. Let us explore the ways in which we have missed the mark.

1. The False Divide Between "Spiritual" and "Material"

One of the most damaging theological errors in Church history is the artificial separation between the spiritual and the material. In some Christian circles, to speak about wealth, land ownership, business, or governance is treated as unspiritual; as if God is uninterested in these matters. This false dualism has caused believers to retreat from leadership in politics, economics, technology, and science. In the early centuries after Christ, some theological streams, influenced by Greek philosophy, began teaching that the physical world was inferior and that the soul's escape from material existence was the ultimate goal. The implications were devastating: if the physical is deemed "less holy," then why bother ruling it? This thinking contradicted God's own declaration *"...it was very good"* (Genesis 1:31).

Instead of producing rulers who understand how to govern economies, shape culture, and manage resources, the Church began producing religious spectators content to sing about heaven while leaving the earth to be ruled by others.

The Powerless Culture of Local Church Programming

Across much of the modern Church, local programming has become predictable, repetitive, and, in many ways, powerless. Sunday services revolve around preaching, singing, and occasional charity work, but rarely do they equip believers to exercise authority over real-world systems. We have perfected the art of "keeping the saints busy" without empowering them to rule.

Our conferences often emphasize personal blessings and emotional experiences but shy away from equipping people to own land, innovate in business, create wealth, or influence legislation. The effect is a congregation that feels spiritually energized on Sunday but economically, politically, and socially powerless on Monday.

A local church should function as a **Kingdom embassy:** a place where citizens of God's kingdom are trained to expand His rule in their sphere of influence. Instead, many have become spiritual entertainment centers where the most ambitious vision is to build a bigger sanctuary rather than transform the surrounding community.

Neglecting Dominion Has a Cost
When the Church refuses to teach and practice material-world rulership, someone else takes that role and they rarely govern by God's standards. Wealth, land, and influence are never left unclaimed. If the Church refuses to occupy them, the unrighteous will. Proverbs 13:22 says, *"The wealth of the sinner is stored up for the righteous,"* but in practice, much of that wealth remains in unrighteous hands because the righteous have no strategy for claiming it.

This is not just an economic issue, it's a generational one. Without land ownership, we lose control of territory. Without economic power, we lose the ability to fund righteous causes. Without influence in education and law, we lose the ability to protect our children from corrupt ideologies. The Church's silence on dominion is not neutral, it is costly.

From Miracle Power to Maintenance Mode
In the New Testament, Jesus and the apostles regularly demonstrated power over the material realm; multiplying food, calming storms, healing bodies, and even raising the

dead. These miracles were not merely displays of compassion. Rather, they were declarations of authority over creation. They announced that God's kingdom had broken into the physical world.

However, in much of the modern Church, the miraculous has been replaced by maintenance. Instead of expecting supernatural interventions that transform cities and economies, we settle for "safe" prayers that avoid challenging the limits of our faith. The absence of the miraculous in the material realm has made the Church seem irrelevant in a world facing tangible crises of famine, disease, environmental disasters, and economic collapse.

When we stop demonstrating authority over the physical world, we send an unspoken message: our God can save your soul, but He cannot touch your soil.

2. The Theology of Escape

Another inaccurate emphasis that has weakened the Church's material-world influence is the obsession with escape. In some circles, the primary focus is on death and surviving until the rapture, as though our main job is to endure this world until we can leave it. This theology of escape has paralyzed Kingdom advancement. Instead of taking territory, we take cover. Instead of building cities, we bunker down in church basements.

Yet Jesus prayed, *"Your kingdom come, your will be done, on earth as it is in heaven"* (Matthew 6:10). If God intended for His people to abandon the earth to darkness, why would He command us to bring heaven's culture to it? The theology of escape denies the Genesis Mandate, weakens our influence, and hands the world over to those willing to rule it. It confines salvation to the future, when in fact it is all-encompassing because Jesus came to save us even now.

3. Economic Illiteracy in the Pulpit

One of the most glaring inaccuracies in Church culture is the lack of serious economic teaching. While tithes and offerings are frequently preached, there is little emphasis on teaching believers how to create wealth, invest wisely, and control resources. This omission ensures that congregations remain financially dependent on external systems rather than functioning as self-sustaining Kingdom communities.

The Bible is full of economic wisdom; from Joseph's storehouse strategy in Egypt to Solomon's wealth management. Yet many pulpits avoid these topics, choosing instead to preach vague promises of "financial breakthrough" without providing tangible skills or strategies. We pray for God to "transfer the wealth of the wicked" but fail to train believers to steward it when it arrives. We set our expectations on the many mansions in heaven though landownership is biblical.

Land and Legacy Ignored
One of the Bible's most consistent themes is God's concern for His people to own land. From Abraham to Joshua, land possession was a visible sign of covenant blessing. Yet in many modern congregations, there is no teaching on acquiring, developing, and securing territory. Without land, the Church becomes a tenant in the world rather than a landlord.

When we do not own, we are subject to the terms, prices, and policies of those who do. This is why many churches rent facilities they could have purchased decades ago. The absence of a land ownership mindset has left them perpetually dependent.

Cultural Irrelevance Through Withdrawal
By retreating from the arenas of politics, media, education, and law, the Church has allowed secular ideologies to dominate these spheres. We have ceded influence not because God removed it from us, but because we abandoned it. Salt that remains in the shaker will never flavor the food. Instead of training Kingdom legislators, filmmakers, jour-

nalists, and policy makers, we tell our youth to avoid these "worldly" fields. The result is predictable: the enemy fills them with voices hostile to God's kingdom.

The Way Back to Relevance and Power
To correct these painful inaccuracies, the Church must, first, recover a theology of dominion. This means teaching believers that salvation is not just an escape ticket to heaven, but an enlistment into a royal assignment on earth. It means equipping saints to lead in business, government, science, and technology with the same passion they bring to prayer and worship.

We must return to the miraculous. The early Church advanced not just through persuasive preaching, but through undeniable demonstrations of power in the physical world. Modern believers must expect God to act in visible, tangible ways that prove His authority over creation. Finally, the Church must reclaim its voice in cultural conversations. We cannot disciple nations if we refuse to enter the arenas where nations are shaped.

Conclusion: Repenting from a Half-Gospel
The inaccuracies of the modern Church are not minor adjustments in style or preference. They are fundamental errors that distort the very mission of God's people. We have

preached half the gospel, emphasizing salvation of the soul while ignoring the restoration of man's rulership over the material world.

For this, we must repent. Repentance is not merely an emotional apology; it is a change of course. The Church must rise from its comfortable pews, embrace the full scope of the Kingdom mandate, and step back into the role God assigned from the beginning: Rulers of the Material World, operating under His authority, for His glory, and for the benefit of all creation.

Chapter 2

The Original Intent

Before There Was Sin, There Was a Mandate

Before Adam ever sinned, before there was a need for salvation, there was a Kingdom assignment. The very first recorded words of God to mankind were not about worship services, sacrifices, or even moral rules. They were about rulership. Genesis 1:26–28 records the blueprint:

> *"Then God said, 'Let us make man in our image, after our likeness. And let them have dominion over the fish of the sea and over the birds of the heavens and over the livestock and over all the earth and over every creeping thing that creeps on the earth.'"*

From the outset, God's "original intent" was clear:

man was made to manage, govern, and develop the material world under God's supreme authority. This was not an afterthought or a secondary assignment. Dominion is woven into the DNA of humanity.

When you strip away the centuries of theological clutter and religious traditions, the creation account reveals a startling truth: before man ever learned to pray, he was commissioned to rule. Prayer was always meant to be a tool for rulership, not an escape from it.

Heaven's Legal Decree - the Word "Let"

In Genesis 1:26, God uses the phrase "Let us make man…" and "Let them have dominion." The Hebrew text conveys legal force. This is not wishful thinking but a decree. The word "let" functions as a command that releases authority. God could have said, "We will keep dominion in heaven and let man focus only on worship," but He didn't. Instead, He delegated earthly management to human beings. That "let" is the moment heaven signed a legal contract giving humanity jurisdiction over the earth.

This is why, throughout Scripture, God consistently works through human agency to accomplish His will on earth. He gave man the keys and keys imply access, control, and the right to open and shut.

Psalm 8 - Heaven's Commentary on Earth's Rulers

Centuries after Moses recorded the Genesis account, King David sang about the wonder of this original mandate in Psalm 8:

> *"What is man that you are mindful of him, and the son of man that you care for him? Yet you have made him a little lower than the heavenly beings and crowned him with glory and honor. You have given him dominion over the works of your hands; you have put all things under his feet." (Psalm 8:4-6)*

David was stunned that the Creator of galaxies would crown dust-made man with glory and honor and then hand him the keys to creation. He doesn't say, "You allowed him to borrow a few things." He says, "You have put all things under his feet." That's positional language. It's about authority and subjugation.

In biblical thought, what is "under the feet" is under one's control. God intended man to have an operational hierarchy in creation: God over man, man over creation.

Dominion Is Not Domination

The word "dominion" has been abused and misunderstood.

Some have equated it with reckless exploitation, as though God gave man permission to destroy the planet for profit. That is a distortion. Dominion is not domination.

To dominate is to exploit without accountability. To exercise dominion is to govern with stewardship. Adam's assignment to *"work and keep"* the garden (Genesis 2:15) meant cultivating the earth's potential while protecting its integrity. Dominion is rulership on behalf of another; in this case, on behalf of God.

This means every use of creation's resources should align with the Owner's will. Dominion is not permission to pollute rivers, strip mountains, and impoverish nations. It is the responsibility to manage resources so that both humanity and the earth flourish.

Why the Mandate Precedes the Fall

It is significant that the rulership mandate was given before sin entered the world. That means it is part of God's eternal design for humanity, not a temporary task subject to redemption history. Salvation does not remove the mandate, it restores it.

If the only goal of salvation were to get us to heaven, God could have taken Adam and Eve away immediately after the fall. Instead, the story of Scripture is about restoring the relationship with God and reinstating man's role as His representative ruler in the earth.

The Genesis Mandate is permanent. Revelation 5:10 confirms that in the age to come, the redeemed "shall reign on the earth." The bookends of the Bible, Genesis and Revelation, both present man as ruler. The fall interrupted the mandate, but it did not cancel it.

Made in God's Image for a Reason

The Genesis Mandate is inseparable from the statement that man is made in God's image and likeness. This is the qualification for rulership. You cannot govern on God's behalf without reflecting His nature.

Image speaks of nature: God's moral, creative, and rational capacities. Likeness speaks of function: the ability to operate in ways consistent with His will. Being in His image means we have the capacity for justice, mercy, creativity, and vision. Being in His likeness means we can execute these qualities in our governance.

The mandate to rule was not given to animals, angels, or plants. It was given to beings uniquely designed to think, speak, and create like God. This is why Psalm 115:16 says, "The heavens are the Lord's heavens, but the earth he has given to the children of man."

The Scope of the Mandate

Genesis 1:26–28 (ESV) records the most comprehensive statement of man's authority ever issued:

> *"Then God said, 'Let us make man in our image, after our likeness. And let them have dominion over the fish of the sea and over the birds of the heavens and over the livestock and over all the earth and over every creeping thing that creeps on the earth.' So God created man in his own image, in the image of God he created him; male and female he created them. And God blessed them. And God said to them, 'Be fruitful and multiply and fill the earth and subdue it, and have dominion over the fish of the sea and over the birds of the heavens and over every living thing that moves on the earth.'"*

From this passage, we see five distinct realms of rulership:

1. Over the Fish of the Sea

This represents man's authority over the marine world; everything in oceans, seas, rivers, and lakes. This includes fish, aquatic mammals, coral reefs, sea plants, and even microscopic life in water. The marine realm is one of the most resource-rich parts of the planet.

First, God's intent was that man would **harvest the**

wealth of the waters. Fish provide food, industry, and economic trade; seas yield minerals, oil, and transportation routes. Ruling "over the fish" means understanding, managing, and protecting aquatic life for sustained benefit. The fishing nets of Peter and the miraculous catches in Jesus' ministry show God's willingness to intervene in this domain for Kingdom purposes.

Second, dominion here implies **environmental care.** Rulership over the seas does not mean reckless overfishing or pollution. It means aligning harvesting with God's design for balance. The same God who told Jonah about His concern for Nineveh also mentioned the many animals there. God cares about the ecosystems He made.

Third, this domain includes **technological mastery** of marine environments. Shipbuilding, navigation, undersea exploration, and even modern advances like oceanic renewable energy all fall under the category of "fish of the sea" dominion. When believers understand this scope, they realize that controlling shipping lanes or developing sustainable ocean resources is a Kingdom activity, not a secular one.

2. Over the Birds of the Heavens

This domain refers to the airspace above us that includes the birds, insects, and even the atmospheric systems they inhabit. It represents mastery of the skies.

First, it represents **agricultural balance and environmental stewardship.** Birds are essential for food, pollination, seed dispersion, and pest control. A ruler of the material world must understand the ecological role of avian life and ensure that habitats are preserved. Scripture often uses birds as metaphors for spiritual truths, for instance: the eagle's strength, the dove's peace. But in the Genesis Mandate, they are also an economic and environmental resource.

Second, this includes **atmospheric management.** God's control over weather in Scripture, from Elijah stopping the rain to Jesus calming the storm, points to authority over climate systems. While humans cannot create weather at will in our natural capacity, the Church should not be ignorant of how prayer, technology, and stewardship can influence the stability of the air we breathe and the skies we navigate.

Third, "birds of the heavens" speaks of **aviation and air transport.** The ability to design aircraft, navigate air routes, and manage airspace is a fulfillment of this mandate. The Wright brothers, whether they knew it or not, tapped into a God-given domain when they pioneered human flight. Dominion here includes both the natural birds and the technological mastery of their realm.

3. Over the Livestock

This realm covers animals, both wild and domesticated, agricultural industries, and the production of food and textiles.

First, "livestock" represents **food, security and agricultural dominance.** Cattle, sheep, goats, and other domesticated animals have been essential to human survival and economic growth throughout history. Dominion here means developing systems of breeding, feeding, and protecting herds in ways that align with God's provision plan for humanity.

Second, livestock rulership connects to **economic wealth and trade.** In biblical times, wealth was measured in flocks and herds. Job's prosperity was listed in livestock numbers before it was ever expressed in silver and gold. This shows that control over agricultural production is a major form of economic influence. Believers who understand this can see ranching, farming, and agricultural entrepreneurship as expressions of their God-given rulership.

Third, this realm includes **innovation in industry.** Wool, leather, milk, and meat all come from livestock, feeding entire manufacturing sectors. Dominion means improving production without compromising animal welfare, creating efficient systems, and ensuring communities have sustainable resources. This is part of exercising the

Genesis Mandate in the modern era.

4. Over All the Earth

This is the broadest domain: governance over land, resources, geography, and societal structures.

First, "over all the earth" includes **territorial authority.** In Scripture, land ownership was central to covenant blessing. God promised Abraham land, led Israel to a promised territory, and defended that inheritance through generations. Rulership here means securing and developing territory for righteous purposes.

Second, this phrase encompasses **management of natural resources**: forests, minerals, oil, soil, and all renewable and non-renewable assets. Nations rise or fall based on how they manage their resources. The believer's mandate is to ensure these resources are developed in ways that bless communities, not just enrich elites.

Third, it speaks of **societal governance**. Ruling "over all the earth" implies setting laws, policies, and systems that reflect God's justice and mercy. This is why righteous leadership in politics, education, and law is not optional for the Church. It is embedded in the original blueprint of creation.

5. Over Every Creeping Thing That Creeps on the Earth

This domain includes small creatures; insects, reptiles, and other ground-level life forms. It also symbolically represents control over the smallest and potentially most harmful forces in the earth.

First, this covers **public health and pest control.** Many diseases in human history have been transmitted by "creeping things" like mosquitoes, rodents, parasites, for example. Dominion means researching, managing, and eliminating harmful infestations that disrupt the ecosystem and threaten human life.

Second, it represents **scientific mastery at the micro-level.** This ties directly to biology, microbiology, and medical research. Understanding and controlling bacteria, viruses, and microscopic organisms falls squarely under the Genesis Mandate. These "small things" can have massive impacts on human society just as the COVID-19 pandemic revealed.

Third, it includes **symbolic authority over persistent irritants and threats**. In the natural world, creeping things are often nuisances; in the spiritual and social world, they represent recurring problems that undermine progress. The mandate to rule over them means refusing to let the smallest forces derail the big purposes of God in the earth.

This is comprehensive. God essentially said, "Every physical system on this planet is under your jurisdiction." That means from the soil under our feet to the weather patterns above our heads, man was intended to govern.

Humanity's Mandate: Fruitful, Multiply, Fill, Subdue, Have Dominion

Gen 1:27-28 AMP says:
> 27 So God created man in His own image, in the image and likeness of God He created him; male and female He created them. 28 And God blessed them and said to them, Be fruitful, multiply, and fill the earth, and subdue it [using all its vast resources in the service of God and man]; and have dominion over the fish of the sea, the birds of the air, and over every living creature that moves upon the earth.

In this passage, God gives humanity five core commands; a sequence that reveals how dominion is established and maintained. These are not poetic niceties. They are strategic instructions for governing the material world.

1. Be Fruitful

To be fruitful means to produce results from what God has given you. It's the refusal to let potential remain dormant. In agriculture, fruitfulness is the natural outcome of healthy growth. In human calling, it is the deliberate outcome of cultivating gifts, resources, and opportunities. Fruitfulness is the antidote to waste. Every seed, whether a skill, an idea, a relationship, or a piece of land, carries within it the potential for multiplication, but only if it is cultivated.

Fruitfulness also speaks to **quality, not just quantity.** Producing a lot of mediocre work is not the biblical standard. God's creation was both abundant and excellent. When believers embrace fruitfulness, they commit to producing results that bear the excellence of their Creator. This applies to art, business, governance, education - every domain in which we operate.

On a spiritual level, fruitfulness is evidence of alignment with God's will. Jesus said in John 15:8, *"By this my Father is glorified, that you bear much fruit and so prove to be my disciples."* A fruitful believer demonstrates Kingdom legitimacy in both the spiritual and material arenas. If your faith is real, it should produce visible, beneficial change around you.

2. Multiply

Multiplication goes beyond fruitfulness. It is the replication of what is produced. If fruitfulness is about results, multiplication is about scaling those results so they impact more people, places, and generations. In the natural order, multiplication ensures survival and expansion; in Kingdom order, it ensures influence and legacy.

This principle applies to wealth, wisdom, and works. A believer who multiplies takes the initial results God has given and creates systems, processes, or mentorship pathways so that others can produce similar results. This is why Paul told Timothy, *"What you have heard from me… entrust to faithful men who will be able to teach others also"* (2 Timothy 2:2). Multiplication preserves and expands influence.

Spiritually and materially, multiplication also requires vision. You cannot multiply what you have if you only think about yourself. The command to multiply forces us to think generationally; to build something that will outlive us and continue to bless the earth after we are gone.

3. Fill the Earth

Filling the earth means extending the presence, principles, and culture of God to every region. This is not just about human population growth; it's about saturating every corner of the planet with Kingdom influence. Eden was never meant to remain a single location. It was the prototype for the entire earth.

This command requires **movement and expansion**. It confronts the human tendency to settle into comfort zones. God's people are not meant to cluster in small enclaves while leaving vast territories untouched by Kingdom order. Filling the earth means establishing righteous governance, economic stability, and cultural development in every sphere and geography.

Historically, the failure to obey this command has led to territorial losses. When Israel refused to fully possess the Promised Land, enemy nations remained as thorns in their side. The principle is timeless: what you fail to fill will eventually be filled by someone else, and often by forces opposed to God's purposes.

4. Subdue It

To subdue means to bring under control that which resists. It is the act of bringing chaotic elements into order. In the Genesis context, it implies confronting anything in creation that hinders God's intended harmony and productivity.

Subduing involves both **force and wisdom**. It is not mindless aggression but strategic mastery. A farmer subdues wild land through cultivation. A leader subdues corruption through righteous laws. A scientist subdues disease through research and treatment. This command acknowledges that not everything in creation will cooperate automatically some things must be brought into alignment through decisive action.

In the spiritual realm, subduing extends to resisting and overturning the influence of the kingdom of darkness in human affairs. Wherever there is injustice, oppression, or disorder, the sons of God are called to step in and bring order. Subduing is the Kingdom's way of saying, "Chaos will not have the last word here."

5. Have Dominion

Dominion is the ongoing governance of what has been subdued. It is the sustained management of the domains entrusted to us. This is not a one-time victory but a continuous stewardship that preserves order, multiplies resources, and advances God's purposes.

Dominion requires **structures and systems.** Without governance structures, victories fade and gains are lost. This is why Joseph's leadership in Egypt was not just about storing grain, it was about creating an administrative system that maintained prosperity over years of famine. Dominion ensures that blessings are not temporary.

Ultimately, dominion is a reflection of God's rule through human agents. It is not a license for selfish exploitation but a mandate to manage the material world as an extension of heaven's values. It means governing in such a way that when people see our systems, cities, businesses, and lands, they catch a glimpse of the King we represent.

This is not a casual suggestion; it is a royal commissioning. Every verb is active and progressive. Rulership is not static. It requires creativity, innovation, and vigilance.

Necessary Equipment for Rulership: Glory and Honor

Psalm 8:2-9 says,

> "Nursing infants gurgle choruses about you; toddlers shout the songs That drown out enemy talk, and silence atheist babble. 3 I look up at your macro-skies, dark and enormous, your handmade sky-jewelry, Moon and stars mounted in their settings. 4 Then I look at my micro-self and wonder, Why do you bother with us? Why take a second look our way? 5 Yet we've so narrowly missed being gods, bright with Eden's dawn light. 6 You put us in charge of your handcrafted world, repeated to us your Genesis-charge, 7 Made us lords of sheep and cattle, even animals out in the wild, 8 Birds flying and fish swimming, whales singing in the ocean deeps. 9 God, brilliant Lord, your name echoes around the world."
>
> MSG

Psalm 8 adds an important perspective necessary to the success of the Genesis Mandate: God crowned man with glory and honor before giving him dominion. Glory is the manifestation of God's nature in us; honor is the recognition of our value and authority. Together, they form the "equipment" for rulership.

You cannot rule effectively if you do not carry glory (divine character) and honor (legitimate authority). This is why sin damaged our ability to rule. It tarnished glory and undermined honor. Redemption restores both, re-qualifying us for the original mandate.

The Mandate Was Global from the Start

God did not limit Adam's rule to the Garden of Eden. Eden was headquarters; the model. But the command was to fill the earth. God expected Adam's descendants to extend the order, beauty, and productivity of Eden to every corner of the globe.

This global perspective is important because it shows that God's intent was never for His people to be localized, powerless enclaves. His plan was for them to shape civilizations. The Great Commission is simply the Genesis Mandate renewed: Go into all the world, bring it under Kingdom order.

The Fall as a Transfer of Management

When Adam disobeyed, he did not lose the earth. God did not give it to Satan. Psalm 24:1 says, "The earth is the Lord's and the fullness of it…" However, Adam did lose the right to govern it according to God's will. By submitting to the serpent's deception, he effectively handed operational control to a rebellious spiritual power.

This is why Jesus refers to Satan as the "prince of this world" (John 12:31). This is not because Satan owns the earth, but because he illegally occupies the management role Adam forfeited. The rest of Scripture is the story of God reclaiming earth's governance through covenant, law, and ultimately through Christ.

Jesus as the Second Adam Restoring the Mandate
When Jesus came, He did not only come to forgive sins; He came to restore man's authority. This is why He demonstrated mastery over every element listed in the Genesis Mandate. He commanded fish into nets, spoke to storms, multiplied bread, and healed bodies.

In Matthew 28:18, He declares, "All authority in heaven and on earth has been given to me." That is the Genesis Mandate reclaimed. When He commissions His disciples, He essentially says, "Now extend this reclaimed authority into every nation."

Why the Church Must Return to the Original Intent
If the Church ignores the Genesis Mandate and Psalm 8 commentary, we are essentially rejecting God's first words to humanity. The gospel is not complete until it restores man to his original role as earth's governor under heaven's

King.

This means believers must stop seeing themselves as passive residents waiting for heaven and start seeing themselves as active rulers shaping the future. Our assignment is not just to survive in the world, but to govern it in alignment with God's purposes.

The Practical Implications

Restoring the original intent of God's Genesis Mandate has tangible, measurable effects in the modern world. This is not just theory or ancient history. It is a living assignment for believers today.

How the Mandate Plays Out in Practice

1. Economic Influence - Creating Systems that Bless Communities

Economic influence begins with the understanding that wealth is a tool, not an idol. God entrusts resources to His people so they can build systems that bless entire communities, not just individuals. In biblical history, Joseph's economic strategy in Egypt saved both Egyptians and Israelites from famine. His model shows that Kingdom economics is about foresight, stewardship, and equitable distribution.

For believers today, economic influence means building businesses, investment networks, and trade relationships that operate with integrity and generosity. It means rejecting exploitative practices and instead using profit to fund education, healthcare, and community development. It's not enough to earn money; the call is to direct capital toward redemptive purposes.

This influence also extends to policy. Those with economic power shape laws, set labor standards, and determine how resources are allocated. When believers operate from positions of financial strength, they can ensure that economic systems reflect biblical values of justice, fairness, and stewardship. Economic dominion means believers are not at the mercy of corrupt systems they build systems that reflect the Kingdom.

2. Territorial Stewardship - Owning and Managing Land Responsibly

Land ownership is one of the clearest biblical signs of covenant blessing. From Abraham's promised territory to the division of land among Israel's tribes, God repeatedly linked blessing to the possession of land. Territorial stewardship means not only acquiring land but using it in ways that glorify God and serve the community.

In the modern context, territorial stewardship might involve sustainable farming, property development that strengthens local economies, or creating protected spaces for natural habitats. The goal is to make land productive in ways that align with God's creation mandate. When believers own land, they gain control over how it is used, developed, and preserved.

This is not just about agriculture or real estate; it's about jurisdiction. Whoever owns the land sets the rules for its use. If righteous people own and manage territory, they can ensure that it becomes a platform for righteousness, whether that means hosting worship gatherings, building schools, or developing businesses that employ the local community.

3. Cultural Leadership - Shaping Values in Art, Education, and Policy

Culture is one of the most powerful forces in society. It shapes how people think, what they value, and how they behave. Cultural leadership means stepping into the arenas that form culture (the arts, education, media, entertainment, and policy) and intentionally influencing them with Kingdom truth.

In biblical times, Daniel demonstrated cultural leadership in Babylon. He worked within a pagan system but maintained his convictions, influencing policy and earning the respect of kings. Today, cultural leadership might mean producing films that carry moral clarity, writing curriculum that aligns with biblical principles, or crafting policies that defend family values and religious freedom.

Believers cannot afford to retreat from culture. The Genesis Mandate calls us to fill the earth, which includes filling its cultural spaces with godly values. If the Church withdraws, other voices will fill the vacuum, often promoting ideas that erode biblical truth. Cultural leadership ensures that the narrative shaping society is consistent with the Creator's design.

4. Scientific Innovation - Discovering and Applying Creation's Potential

Science is not the enemy of faith; it is the study of God's handiwork. The Genesis Mandate to subdue the earth implies a call to explore, understand, and harness creation's laws for the good of humanity. From metallurgy in Tubal-Cain's time to Solomon's architectural marvels, Scripture celebrates technological and scientific advancement when it is used for righteous purposes.

Scientific innovation includes medical research, engineering breakthroughs, clean energy solutions, and technological developments that improve quality of life. Believers should be on the front lines of these fields, not absent from them. Our faith should inspire curiosity, creativity, and a desire to solve real-world problems.

When Kingdom-minded scientists, engineers, and innovators lead the way, they ensure that discovery is guided by ethics, stewardship, and compassion. Without such influence, technological progress can be twisted into tools of exploitation or destruction. Scientific dominion is not about controlling nature for selfish ends but about unlocking its potential in harmony with God's design.

5. Environmental Care - Protecting Ecosystems While Using Them Productively

Environmental care is not a modern political agenda, it is part of the original job description for humanity. Adam was told to "work and keep" the garden (Genesis 2:15), which meant both cultivating it for productivity and protecting it from harm. Dominion is not a license to destroy; it is a mandate to maintain balance.

In today's context, environmental care might involve reforestation, responsible fishing, waste reduction, and renewable energy initiatives. It requires a mindset that sees creation as a trust from God, to be preserved for future generations. The righteous ruler of the material world recognizes that the earth is the Lord's, and we are accountable for how we treat it.

Believers engaged in environmental stewardship can counter the extremes of both reckless exploitation and anti-human environmentalism. The Kingdom approach seeks to maximize human flourishing without compromising the integrity of the ecosystems God created. This kind of care reflects God's heart for both people and the planet.

Recovering the Blueprint

The Genesis Mandate and Psalm 8 make it undeniable: man was created to rule the material world on God's behalf. This is not arrogance; it is obedience to the Creator's assignment. Dominion is not about ego but stewardship.

If we are to fulfill our Kingdom calling, we must recover the blueprint. The Church must preach not just about heaven but about the earth we are commissioned to govern. We must teach believers how to translate spiritual authority into practical rulership that benefits society and honors God.

The original intent has not changed. It is time for the people of God to reclaim their crown. Let us further explore the elements that make up the material world before we delve into the biblical case studies that further support the Genesis Mandate.

Chapter 3

The Vast Expanse of the Material World

What God Placed Under Human Stewardship

Creation is not an abstract idea in Scripture. It is rock and river, atmosphere and ore, valley and voltage. When God said, "Let them have dominion," He entrusted to humanity the visible, tangible fabric of the world; the matter that feeds us, moves us, shelters us, and empowers our civilizations. This chapter surveys that fabric. We will look closely at the architecture of matter (solids, liquids, and gases), then walk the reader through a curated treasury of forty-eight strategic minerals and materials that anchor modern life. Throughout, we will hold to one thesis: God intends the material world to be ruled wisely by people made in His image.

The Bible's Material Imagination

Scripture never treats matter as disposable. It calls it "very good." Job 28 reverberates with the audacity of human mining: "Man puts an end to darkness; he searches out to the farthest limit… he opens shafts in a valley away from where anyone lives." The chapter reads like a documentary of ancient engineering: ore sorted from rock, veins traced through mountains, stones weighed, metals smelted. Deuteronomy 8 names a land "whose stones are iron and out of whose hills you can dig copper." The biblical imagination assumes people will learn, extract, shape, and deploy what God hid in the earth, under God, for good.

Dominion, then, is not a right to ravage but a call to reveal. Our task is to bring latent potential into the light: to convert the gift of matter into flourishing for people and praise for God.

The Architecture of Matter: Solids, Liquids, and Gases

The material world presents itself in three everyday states, solids, liquids, and gases, each with distinct rules we must learn and steward.

Solids: Structure, Storage, and Strength

Solids hold shape. They store energy, bear loads, form tools, and build homes. From timber and stone to steel and silicon, solids give civilization its bones. To rule solids is to understand strength, fracture, fatigue, hardness, and heat; to design bridges that don't fall, perform surgeries that use bio-compatible alloys, and circuits etched into wafers so small that millions fit on a fingernail. Dominion over solids includes the humble (brick) and the exquisite (diamond-tipped drills), the ancient (lime mortar) and the cutting edge (graphene research). In biblical categories: altars were built of stone, temples framed by cedar. Today, hospitals rise on reinforced concrete, and clean rooms shelter microchips. Solids are the scaffolding of human purpose. (A detailed list of the The Earth's Treasury of Materials and Minerals can be found at the end of this section.)

Liquids: Flow, Life, and Leverage
Liquids take the shape of their container and move under gravity and pressure. Water is the heartbeat of agriculture, hygiene, energy, and life itself. Dominion here includes aquifers and canals, dams and desalination, irrigation and flood control. It includes the chemistry of solvents and solutions, pharmaceuticals and fuels. *"He leads me beside still waters"* is poetry, while managing reservoirs and rivers is policy. When we steward liquids, cities drink, crops thrive, power flows, and disease retreats.

Gases: Breath, Buoyancy, and Balance

Gases expand to fill space. Air carries sound and weather, planes and pollen. The atmosphere's delicate composition, nitrogen, oxygen, water vapor, trace gases, makes life possible. Dominion over gases means understanding climate and combustion, pressure and propulsion; it means clean air standards, aviation safety, refrigeration, and the emerging hydrogen economy. Biblically, God "makes the winds His messengers." Practically, we manage the winds for flight, turbines, and comfort. Wise rulership honors the physics of the sky while defending the dignity of those who breathe it.

The Earth's Treasury: 48 Strategic Minerals and Materials

Below is a concise tour of forty-eight minerals/materials that anchor modern life. Each entry names core uses, not to idolize resources, but to illustrate what it means to "subdue" and "have dominion" with intelligence and ethics.

1. Iron (hematite, magnetite): Backbone of steel for buildings, bridges, rails, machinery. Without iron, industrial strength collapses.
2. Copper (chalcopyrite): Premier electrical conductor for power grids, wiring, motors, and plumbing.

3. Aluminum (bauxite): Lightweight metal for aircraft, vehicles, packaging, and conductive busbars.
4. Gold: Non-corroding conductor in electronics; monetary reserve; surgical and dental uses.
5. Silver: Highest electrical/thermal conductivity; solar cells; medical antimicrobial applications.
6. Platinum: Catalysts for refining and chemical synthesis; medical implants; fuel cells.
7. Palladium: Automotive catalytic converters; electronics; hydrogen storage research.
8. Nickel: Stainless steel alloying; batteries; corrosion-resistant equipment.
9. Cobalt: High-energy batteries; superalloys for jet engines; medical radioisotopes.
10. Lithium: Rechargeable batteries powering devices, vehicles, and grid storage.
11. Graphite: Electrodes; lubricants; battery anodes; heat management.
12. Silicon (quartz): Semiconductors; solar photovoltaics; glass; silicones.
13. Titanium (rutile, ilmenite): Aerospace alloys; medical implants; pigments (TiO_2).

14. Chromium (chromite): Stainless steel; plating; corrosion resistance.
15. Manganese: Steel toughening; dry-cell batteries; fertilizers.
16. Molybdenum: High-strength, high-temperature steels; catalysts; lubricants.
17. Tungsten (wolframite, scheelite): Cutting tools; drill bits; high-temperature filaments.
18. Vanadium: Alloy for strong, light steels; grid-scale redox flow batteries.
19. Tin (cassiterite): Lead-free solders; plating; bronze alloy.
20. Lead (galena): Batteries; radiation shielding; specialized glass.
21. Zinc (sphalerite): Galvanizing steel; brass; die-casting; health supplements.
22. Uranium: Dense fuel for nuclear power; research isotopes; naval propulsion.
23. Thorium: Prospective nuclear fuel; high-temperature ceramics and optics.
24. Neodymium (rare earth): Powerful permanent magnets for motors, wind turbines, audio.
25. Dysprosium (rare earth): Heat-resistant magnets, enabling high-temp motor perfor-

mance.

26. Lanthanum (rare earth): Petrochemical catalysts; camera lenses; batteries.

27. Cerium (rare earth): Glass polishing; catalysts; self-cleaning alloys.

28. Praseodymium (rare earth): Magnets; lasers; aviation alloys.

29. Yttrium (rare earth): Phosphors in LEDs; high-temp ceramics; medical applications.

30. Tantalum (tantalite/coltan): Electronics capacitors; surgical implants; corrosion-proof equipment.

31. Niobium: Superconductors; steel micro-alloying for pipelines and structures.

32. Beryllium (beryl): Ultra-light stiff alloys for aerospace, satellites, precision instruments.

33. Boron (borates): Borosilicate glass; detergents; fiberglass; agriculture.

34. Phosphate (apatite): Fertilizers sustaining global agriculture; food processing.

35. Potash (K salts): Fertilizer balancing soil nutrients; industrial brines.

36. Sulfur: Sulfuric acid (industrial workhorse); fertilizers; pharmaceuticals.

37. Gypsum: Drywall; cement retarder; soil conditioning.

38. Limestone (calcite): Cement; steel making flux; agriculture; water treatment.

39. Clay (kaolinite): Ceramics; paper coating; pharmaceuticals; cosmetics.

40. Feldspar: Glass and ceramics flux; fillers in paints and plastics.

41. Mica: Electrical insulation; heat barriers; cosmetics pearlescence.

42. Talc: Fillers; ceramics; paints; food-grade anti-caking.

43. Barite: Drilling mud weighting; medical imaging; radiation shielding.

44. Fluorite: Steel flux; fluorochemicals (refrigerants, polymers); optics.

45. Halite (rock salt): Chemical feedstock (chlor-alkali); food salt; de-icing.

46. Zeolite: Ion exchange; water softening; petrochemical catalysis; odor control.

47. Garnet: Industrial abrasives; waterjet cutting; filtration media.

48. Diamond: Cutting, drilling, polishing; heat spreaders in high-power electronics.

This is only a sampling of what God hid in the crust. The point is not to memorize the list; it is to recognize the mandate: learn how the world works so you can bless the world well.

Dominion Over Matter

The material world has been defined, however it is imperative that we understand how to properly steward it.

Solids: Dominion Over the Firm Foundations

Ruling solids begins with understanding materials properties and supply chains. A city's strength is not only in its theology but in its concrete, steel, timber, and brick; in the quality of its roads and rails; in the reliability of its transformers and turbines. Consider three arenas:

> **1. Built Environments:** The wise ruler knows why rebar is embedded in concrete (tension vs. compression), why seismic joints matter, and how materials fail. This is not trivia, it is justice. Poorly built schools collapse on the poor. Good dominion designs structures that outlast storms and serve generations.
>
> **2. Tools and Machines:** The difference between hardened steel and high-speed steel, or between carbide and diamond tooling, translates into productivity and safety. Dominion

puts the right material in the right task, extracting more value with less waste.

3. Electronics and Optics: Silicon wafers, rare-earth magnets, copper traces, and glass fibers undergird the digital economy. To rule here is to understand purity, doping, bandwidth, interference, and thermal management; and to fight for ethical sourcing that does not exploit workers or scar lands.

Solids also implicate **land** directly: soil science (texture, structure, fertility), erosion control, and geotechnical stability. A righteous people plant windbreaks, terrace hillsides, stabilize slopes, and replenish topsoil. Abuse the soil and you export your future harvests into the sea.

Liquids: Dominion Over the Waters That Sustain Life

Water governance is civilization 101. Irrigation made ancient empires possible; modern basins and aquifers make megacities possible. Dominion over liquids includes:

1. Water Security: Capture (reservoirs, cisterns), purification (filtration, chlorination, advanced membranes), distribution (pumps, pressure zoning), and reuse (graywater, recharge). Every drought and flood is an exam in stewardship: did we plan, build, and maintain wisely?

2. Public Health: Wastewater treatment breaks disease cycles; storm water systems prevent contamination. Dominion sets standards for rivers and beaches, protects wetlands that buffer floods, and restores riparian corridors that keep ecosystems alive.

3. Liquid Energy and Chemistry: Fuels, lubricants, refrigerants, and solvents all obey rules of viscosity, volatility, and reactivity. Wise rulers regulate safely, innovate alternatives, and reduce leaks and losses. They deploy district cooling, thermal storage, and industrial symbiosis to save energy and money.

Dominion is not water-wealthy landscaping in deserts; it is matching crops to climates, replacing leaky mains, pricing water justly, and ensuring that the widow on a fixed income and the child in an informal settlement both drink as safely as the governor.

Gases: Dominion Over the Air We Share

Air is shared, and shared things demand shared wisdom.

1. Clean Air: Combustion by-products, dust,

and volatile compounds harm lungs and shorten lives. Dominion sets emissions limits, monitors air quality, enforces compliance, and transitions fleets to cleaner power. It is a moral act when children breathe easier.

2. Flight and Weather: Aviation requires mastery of pressure, lift, turbulence, and icing. Air traffic management is an exercise in order and trust. Weather services save lives by predicting storms and heat waves; wise rulers build early-warning systems and shelters.

3. Thermal Comfort and Refrigeration: Cooling protects vaccines, preserves food, and saves lives in heat waves. Dominion chooses refrigerants with lower environmental impact, maintains equipment to prevent leakage, designs buildings that require less cooling, and ensures access for the vulnerable.

Stewarding gases also includes industrial gases (oxygen for steel making and hospitals; nitrogen for inerting and fertilizers; hydrogen for refining and potential clean energy). The atmosphere is our commons; faithful rulers keep it fit for life.

From Ore to Opportunity: Supply Chains and Justice

Dominion over the material world cannot ignore the **human and moral** dimensions of extraction and manufacturing. Mines can create livelihoods or misery. Smelters can lift towns or poison them. Electronics can empower education or encourage entertainment that distracts. The righteous ruler insists on transparent supply chains, fair wages, safe conditions, reclamation of mined land, and community consent.

Biblically, dominion is covenantal: the land must be allowed to rest; boundaries must be honored; weights and measures must be just. Practically, this translates into environmental impact assessments, tailings dam safety, remediation funds, and standards that keep profit from devouring people.

Learning the Language of Matter

If believers are to lead, we must become fluent in the world's physical grammar. That means:

- **Scientific Literacy:** Knowing why alloys resist corrosion, how membranes filter water, what makes a magnet strong, or why certain soils swell.
- **Systems Thinking:** Seeing how a decision in

mining affects rivers, how a dam alters sediment, how a battery supply chain touches multiple continents.
- **Economic Wisdom:** Understanding markets, logistics, recycling, and the lifetime cost of materials, not just upfront price.
- **Design for Stewardship:** Prioritizing durability, repairability, and circularity; keeping materials in use longer, recovering them at end-of-life, and reducing waste.

When the righteous understand materials, they can craft policies, companies, projects, and products that extend the goodness of creation instead of eroding it.

The Theological Horizon: Why Matter Matters
Dominion over matter is not a detour from spirituality; it is an expression of it. We worship a Creator who entered creation in flesh and blood, who ate fish and baked bread, who calmed winds and walked on waves. The Incarnation is God's endorsement of the material as worthy of redemption and rule. The resurrection body is not vapor; it is transformed matter. The future vision is not souls floating in clouds; it is a renewed earth where the nations bring their glory in.

Therefore, Christians should be the most serious stewards of matter on the planet, primarily because we know its Maker, share His image, and carry His mandate.

Practical Pathways for Kingdom Rulership in the Material World

1. Map Your Territory: Inventory the solids, liquids, and gases that define your region: soils, quarries, forests, rivers, aquifers, winds. Identify risks (drought, flood, landslide) and opportunities (industrial clusters, logistics, clean energy).

2. Pick a Domain and Specialize: Metallurgy, water engineering, building science, environmental health, materials finance. Choose a lane and gain mastery. Dominion requires competence.

3. Build Coalitions: Industry, government, church, academy, and community must collaborate. Secure social license for projects. Share benefits.

4. Design for the Poor: Build with the last, least, and lost in mind: low-cost clean water, cool roofs, clean cookstoves, resilient housing, reliable transit, affordable power.

5. Close the Loop: Promote recycling of metals, safe e-waste processing, construction material reuse, nutrient recovery. Waste is often a sign of failed dominion.

6. Teach the Next Generation: Put Job 28 beside a materials lab; Deuteronomy 8 beside a field trip to a water plant. Train saints to love God and to lay asphalt right, pour concrete well, solder cleanly, and test water faithfully.

Dominion's Ethic: Power With Restraint

The more we can do to matter, the more we must decide not to do. Authority must be yoked to humility. The land must not be stripped bare for vanity; rivers must not be sacrificed for momentary profit; neighborhoods must not be poisoned so distant shareholders can cash out. Power is safe only when it is cruciform; shaped by the self-giving love of Christ.

This is why dominion is best exercised by people who worship: worshipers remember they are not owners but trustees, not gods but images, not takers but givers. They measure success not only in GDP and gigawatts but in justice and joy.

A World Worth Governing

The material world is vast: metals that carry current, stones that carry loads, waters that carry life, and winds that carry seed and song. God placed this world under human feet, not to be trampled but to be tended; not to be feared but to be formed; not to be ignored but to be intelligently, ethically, and worshipfully ruled.

When the Church reclaims this mandate, cities become safer, homes stronger, air cleaner, water sweeter, farms wiser, and economies fairer. People see our good works. They see the bridges that stand, grids that hum, wells that flow and they glorify our Father in heaven. That is dominion done right: matter becoming mercy, resources becoming righteousness, and creation answering, at last, to sons and daughters who know why it exists and what it is for.

By reclaiming the Genesis Mandate, we are positioned to have a stake in the wealth of the entire earth.

Total Global Wealth from Financial and Household Assets

According to the **UBS Global Wealth Report 2025,** private (household) wealth globally is estimated at **$471 trillion,** capturing over 92% of global wealth (United States of America). Other estimates align similarly:

- The World Bank and Credit Suisse report around

$454 trillion in household wealth (Axios).

- McKinsey's analysis places worldwide net worth at around **$520 trillion** in real assets, including infrastructure, machinery, buildings, natural resources, and intellectual property (McKinsey & Company).

Inclusive Wealth: A Broader Measure

The **World Bank's "Changing Wealth of Nations"** initiative considers broader definitions; incorporating produced capital, natural capital, human capital, and financial assets to assess sustainability. Although precise global figures are not fully broken out in recent summary sources, this approach often yields totals significantly higher when compared to household wealth alone (World Bank).

Ecosystem Services: The Hidden Annual Value

Beyond stored wealth, Earth's ecosystems deliver immense ongoing value. Estimates place the **annual economic value of global ecosystem services** between **$33 trillion** (1997 baseline) and up to **$125 trillion** per year by 2011 (Wikipedia). While this isn't "wealth" in the conventional sense, it reflects the immense, continuous provisioning power of the planet.

Summary Table

Category	Estimated Value
Household & Financial Wealth	~$450–$520 trillion
Produced + Natural + Human Capital (Inclusive Wealth)	Potentially much higher, but no global figure in summary.
Ecosystem Services (annual value)	~$33–$125 trillion/year

Final Takeaway

Based on available data, the earth's entire worth according to financial and tangible assets (homes, infrastructure, natural resources) reside in the $450–$520 trillion range. When accounting for ecosystem services and natural capital, the planet delivers tens of trillions of dollars annually in unseen, but vital value.

The world and all that dwell therein have been given to righteous humanity. It is the inheritance of those who are heirs of God and joint heirs with Jesus Christ.

Chapter 4

ଔ

Patriarchs, Covenants, and Lands

Biblical Case Studies in Possessing Territory
From Genesis to Joshua, God repeatedly links His covenant blessings to the tangible possession of land. The promises of God to His chosen servants were rarely abstract; they were grounded in geography, soil, borders, and inheritance. Land was not just a backdrop for Bible stories. It was the physical evidence of divine covenant, the stage upon which God's purposes unfolded. In the lives of the patriarchs and leaders of Israel, we see a consistent theme: the **possession of land is both a sign and a tool of Kingdom rulership.**

Abraham - Called by God and Promised Land as a Sign of Covenant
Abraham's journey begins with a land command. In Gene-

sis 12:1–2, God says:

> *"Go from your country and your kindred and your father's house to the land that I will show you. And I will make of you a great nation..."*

From the start, God ties Abraham's destiny to geography. The land was not just a location, it was a covenant marker. God didn't promise him a vague spiritual blessing. He promised territory. In Genesis 13:14–15, God makes the covenant even more explicit: *"Lift up your eyes... all the land that you see I will give to you and to your offspring forever."*

For Abraham, the land represented more than property. It represented divine ownership transferred through covenant. Every step he took on that soil was a prophetic act of possession. Even when he did not own the land outright, he moved in faith as though it already belonged to him because God had decreed it. His purchase of the cave of Machpelah (Genesis 23:8-20) to bury Sarah was more than a burial plot. It was a legal foothold in the Promised Land, anchoring his descendants' future claim.

Isaac - Re-digging Wells and Staking Claims

Isaac inherited his father's covenant but had to fight to maintain and expand it. Genesis 26 records a season of famine in which Isaac sowed in the land and reaped a hundredfold. But what stands out most in his story is the re-digging of his father's wells that the Philistines had stopped up.

Wells in the ancient world were not just water sources. They were legal claims to territory. Whoever controlled the water controlled the land. By reopening the wells, Isaac was making a bold territorial statement: "What my father possessed under covenant, I will reclaim and protect."

His persistence was met with resistance, but Isaac did not abandon the fight. Each well he reopened or dug was named. There was Esek (dispute), Sitnah (opposition), and finally Rehoboth (room); marking the progression from conflict to divine enlargement. Isaac's life teaches us that covenant possession is not maintained passively. It must be defended and actively reestablished in each generation.

Jacob - Acquiring Territory Through Divine Strategy

Jacob's story is one of transformation and strategy. From the moment he fled from Esau, God began to shape him into a man who could inherit and manage territory. At Bethel, God reaffirmed the covenant given to Abraham and Isaac, promising him land and descendants.

Jacob's path to possession was unconventional. He did not initially seize land through conquest. Instead, he acquired influence and wealth through divine strategy and labor while under Laban's authority. His breeding strategy for the flocks (Genesis 30) was not mere cunning, it was divine insight that increased his holdings until he became exceedingly prosperous.

Upon his return to Canaan, Jacob purchased land near Shechem (Genesis 33:19.) This act was significant: it was the first recorded purchase of territory by Jacob himself, establishing a direct foothold for his descendants. Jacob's story reminds us that land possession can come through wisdom, negotiation, and strategic economic positioning, not only through battle.

Joseph - Economic Rulership and Land Preservation in Egypt

Joseph's journey took him far from the land of his fathers, but even in Egypt, the principle of land and rulership held true. Elevated to the role of governor, Joseph implemented a storage and distribution system that preserved both the people and the territory of Egypt during seven years of famine (Genesis 41).

What is remarkable is that Joseph's leadership resulted in Pharaoh acquiring ownership of virtually all the land in Egypt, except that of the priests, consolidating territorial control under a centralized authority. While Joseph acted in service to Pharaoh, his wisdom and governance demonstrated the Kingdom principle of using economic foresight to preserve land and secure national stability.

Even in exile from the Promised Land, Joseph's mind was fixed on covenant territory. Before his death, he made the Israelites swear to carry his bones back to Canaan (Genesis 50:25). This prophetic act declared that the covenant land, not Egypt, was the ultimate inheritance.

Joshua - Leading Israel to Take Possession of the Promised Land

Joshua's mission was the culmination of centuries of covenant promises. His task was not to dream about the land or merely speak of it, it was to take it. In Joshua 1:3, God tells him: *"Every place that the sole of your foot will tread upon I have given to you, just as I promised to Moses."* The language is both legal and prophetic.

Joshua's campaigns were deliberate and strategic. Cities were conquered, territories divided, and tribal allotments assigned. Possession was not instantaneous; it required battle, endurance, and precise obedience to God's instructions. The conquest of Jericho, with its supernatural collapse, set the tone: victory was not by human strength alone but by divine partnership.

Joshua's leadership cemented Israel's identity as a

land-holding nation. The allotment process ensured that each tribe had a permanent inheritance, embedding the principle that covenant blessing is inseparable from tangible territory.

The Consistent Biblical Pattern - God Ties Blessing to Land Possession

From Abraham to Joshua, the pattern is clear: God's blessing consistently includes the possession of land. This is not merely an Old Testament cultural artifact; it is a divine principle. Land represents stability, jurisdiction, and the ability to establish Kingdom culture in a given region. Without land, a people are vulnerable to displacement, dependency, and cultural erasure.

In every covenant renewal, God reaffirms His intention for His people to control territory. Even the New Testament echoes this principle: Jesus speaks of the meek "inheriting the earth" (Matthew 5:5), and Revelation envisions the saints reigning "on the earth" (Revelation 5:10). The covenant is global in scope but always grounded in physical reality.

Land as Legacy, Security, and a Platform for Influence

Land is legacy. It passes from one generation to another, creating continuity and heritage. Abraham's descendants could point to specific soil as evidence of God's faithfulness. This is why losing land in Israel's history was always seen as a tragedy. It represented a break in covenant blessing.

Land is also security. A people without land are at the mercy of landlords, governments, and external powers. They can be displaced at any time. Possession anchors a community and provides a base for self-sufficiency. This is why biblical law guarded against the permanent loss of family land through the Jubilee system described in Leviticus 25:10. God did not want His people perpetually dispossessed.

Finally, land is a platform for influence. Those who own and control territory set the cultural, economic, and legal atmosphere of that space. When the righteous control the land, they can implement systems that reflect justice, mercy, and truth. When the wicked control the land, oppression often follows. The Church must recover the understanding that **owning land is not just an economic advantage, it is a Kingdom mandate.**

Strategic Principles for Possessing Territory
The stories of the patriarchs and leaders of Israel are not just historical narratives, they are blueprints for Kingdom-minded people in every generation. Possessing terri-

tory, whether in the form of land, institutions, or systems, requires both spiritual alignment and practical strategy. Here are key principles drawn from Scripture that can guide modern believers in reclaiming their place as rulers of the material world.

1. Hear and Obey God's Specific Instruction

Every land possession in Scripture begins with a divine word. Abraham was told exactly where to go. Joshua was given precise boundaries. The first step toward possession is receiving and obeying God's specific instruction for your territory. This means prayerfully discerning where God has called you to plant, invest, build, or buy. Without divine direction, you may fight for land God never intended you to have or ignore land He has assigned to you.

Obedience also requires timing. Israel could not take the Promised Land while in Egypt, nor could they take it before the Canaanites' iniquity was complete (Genesis 15:16). Waiting on God's timing ensures that your possession is both lawful and sustainable.

Practical takeaway: Do not rush into territorial acquisition without clear spiritual confirmation. Let your movement be guided by a word from God and confirmed by wise counsel.

2. Secure Legal and Spiritual Title

Biblical possession is both legal and spiritual. Abraham bought the cave of Machpelah even though God had already promised him all the land. Why? Because legal transactions create a public and documented claim that no one can dispute.

In the modern world, this means ensuring that every acquisition is backed by proper documentation, contracts, and governmental recognition. Spiritually, it means consecrating the land to God, dedicating it for righteous purposes, and refusing to let it be used for ungodly ends.

Practical takeaway: Make sure your title deeds are as secure in the courts of men as they are in the courts of heaven. Sanctify what you own so it reflects the One you represent.

3. Confront Resistance with Persistence

Every patriarch faced opposition in their possession journey. Isaac's wells were contested. Jacob had to negotiate with Laban. Joshua faced fortified cities. Territory will not be handed over without a fight, whether that fight is legal, economic, spiritual, or all three.

Persistence means you keep moving forward despite resistance. It means you have the patience to go through bureaucratic processes, the wisdom to negotiate, and the faith to stand in prayer until breakthrough comes. The enemy's strategy is often to exhaust you before you possess the land. Your strategy must be to outlast him.

Practical takeaway: Expect opposition as a normal part of the process. See it as confirmation that your territory has strategic Kingdom value.

4. Develop the Land as a Kingdom Resource

Owning land is only the beginning. Developing it is what maximizes its value. The Promised Land was described as a place flowing with milk and honey, but those resources still had to be cultivated, harvested, and distributed. Land without development is a dormant asset.

Development can take many forms: agriculture, housing, education centers, places of worship, or business ventures. The goal is to make the land productive so it blesses both its owners and the surrounding community.

Practical takeaway: Plan for productivity from day one. Your land should not just be a monument to ownership. It should be a living source of provision.

5. Protect and Preserve for Generations

God's vision for land possession was generational. The laws of inheritance in Israel ensured that land stayed within the family. Even when sold, it had to be returned in the Jubilee year. The idea was clear: land is not just for you, it is for your children's children.

Protecting land means guarding against predatory sales, unsustainable debt, and unjust seizure. Preserving it means keeping it productive and aligned with God's purposes over decades, not just years.

Practical takeaway: Think beyond your lifetime. Set up legal structures, trusts, or stewardship plans that keep your territory in Kingdom hands for generations.

Final Thought on Territorial Dominion
In Scripture, the possession of land was never incidental. It was always intentional. God gives land to establish His will in that space. When His people control territory, they can set the spiritual, cultural, and economic climate. When they neglect it, others impose a foreign agenda.

Recovering the principle of territorial possession is essential if we are to fulfill the Genesis Mandate in our time. As the patriarchs and leaders of Israel demonstrate, the covenant is always tied to geography. And in God's Kingdom economy, owning land is not just about wealth, it's about rulership.

Chapter 5
ᛝ
Jesus: Master of the Material World
The King Who Commands Creation

Introduction: Dominion in Flesh and Blood

In Genesis 1:26–28, God declared that man should have dominion over the earth's creatures, resources, and systems. Yet for centuries after the fall, humanity's capacity to fully exercise that dominion was compromised by sin, ignorance, and the oppression of the enemy. Then came Jesus, "the Word made flesh" (John 1:14), not only to redeem humanity spiritually but also to **model the restored rulership of the material world.**

Jesus' miracles were not random acts of kindness. They were targeted demonstrations of Genesis-level authority, showing that He was the Second Adam (1 Corinthians 15:45), perfectly exercising the dominion mandate. In every realm, solids, liquids, gases, living organisms, and even economic systems, He demonstrated that **creation responds to the voice of its rightful ruler.**

1. Dominion Over Liquids - Turning Water into Wine

Scripture:

> *"Jesus said to them, 'Fill the jars with water.' And they filled them up to the brim. And he said to them, 'Now draw some out and take it to the master of the feast.' So they took it... the master of the feast... said to the bridegroom... 'you have kept the good wine until now.'"* (John 2:7–10 ESV)

Explanation:

At Cana, Jesus took the most basic liquid resource, water, and restructured it into wine of superior quality. This was not sleight of hand; it was molecular transformation. In that moment, hydrogen and oxygen molecules were reordered, infused with complex organic compounds, aromas, and flavors without the natural process of fermentation.

By doing this, Jesus demonstrated:

> 1. *Ownership over the laws of chemistry:* Creation's formulas are subject to its Creator.
> 2. *Ability to bypass time:* Fermentation is a time-bound process; Jesus compressed it into an instant.

3. *Dominion for joy and honor:* This miracle preserved the dignity of the wedding host, showing dominion used for celebration, not just survival.

2. Dominion Over Liquids and Physics - Walking on Water

Scripture:

> "And in the fourth watch of the night he came to them, walking on the sea." (Matthew 14:25 ESV)

Explanation:

The law of gravity dictates that a human body sinks in water without buoyant support. Jesus defied this law by walking on a turbulent sea. He did not use flotation devices. His authority over the physical laws allowed Him to command surface tension itself.

This miracle revealed:

1. *Supremacy over natural laws:* He is not bound by the limitations He created.
2. *Authority over chaos:* In Scripture, the sea often symbolizes chaos, however Jesus literally walked over it.
3. *Faith partnership:* Peter was invited to share in this dominion, showing that believers, too,

can operate in creation's mastery by faith.

3. Dominion Over Gases and Weather - Calming the Storm

Scripture:

> "And he awoke and rebuked the wind and said to the sea, 'Peace! Be still!' And the wind ceased, and there was a great calm." (Mark 4:39 ESV)

Explanation:

Jesus addressed both **wind** (gas movement) and **waves** (liquid motion) as if they were sentient, and they obeyed. Atmospheric pressure systems and oceanic turbulence responded instantly to His voice.

Key revelations:

> 1. *Creation recognizes the Creator's voice.* Winds and waves respond to authority.
> 2. *Rulership in emergencies:* Dominion is not just about comfort, it's about deliverance in crisis.
> 3. *Restoring order to environment:* Genesis 1 began with God bringing order to chaos. Jesus reenacted that here.

4. Dominion Over Biological Systems - Healing the Sick

Scripture:

> "And Jesus stretched out his hand and touched

him, saying, 'I will; be clean.' And immediately the leprosy left him." (Luke 5:13 ESV)

Explanation:
Leprosy is caused by bacterial infection that damages skin, nerves, and tissue. Jesus, without medication, reversed the biological damage instantly. He demonstrated mastery over **cellular regeneration** and **immune restoration.**

This reveals:

> 1. *Authority over disease-causing organisms:* Viruses, bacteria, and parasites are part of "creeping things" under human dominion.
> 2. *Restoration, not just relief:* He didn't just halt the disease, He restored the man's body to wholeness.
> 3. *Cleansing at multiple levels:* In Jewish culture, leprosy caused social and spiritual isolation. Jesus restored physical health, social acceptance, and ceremonial purity.

5. Dominion Over Food Resources - Multiplying Bread and Fish

Scripture:

> "Taking the five loaves and the two fish, he looked up to heaven and said a blessing. Then he broke the loaves and gave them to the dis-

ciples... And they all ate and were satisfied." (Mark 6:41–42 ESV)

Explanation:

Jesus took limited natural resources and caused them to multiply until thousands were fed. This was not mere division of portions. The food itself **materialized in abundance**.

Key lessons:

>1. *Matter can be replicated under divine command.* The same God who spoke worlds into existence can multiply fish and bread.
>2. *Resource creation in scarcity:* Dominion meets human need, not just for survival but in fullness. The scripture declares "they were satisfied."
>3. *Partnership in distribution:* He involved the disciples, teaching them to be agents of miraculous provision.

6. Dominion Over Economics - The Coin in the Fish's Mouth

Scripture:

> *"...go to the sea and cast a hook and take the first fish that comes up, and when you open its mouth you will find a shekel. Take that and*

give it to them for me and for yourself." (Matthew 17:27 ESV)

Explanation:

Jesus orchestrated an economic miracle involving animal behavior and precise timing. Somewhere in the water, a fish took in a coin, but at Jesus' word, Peter caught that exact fish.

This shows:

> 1. *Control over creation's movements:* The fish swam to Peter's hook at the appointed time.
> 2. *Provision that meets obligations:* Dominion addresses practical, even mundane, needs like tax payment.
> 3. *Blending natural and supernatural:* Fishing was natural, the provision was supernatural.

7. Dominion Over Death - Raising the Dead

Scripture:

> "When he had said these things, he cried out with a loud voice, 'Lazarus, come out.' The man who had died came out..." (John 11:43–44 ESV)

Explanation:

Death represents the ultimate limit in the material world;

the cessation of biological function. By reversing death, Jesus demonstrated authority over **biological entropy** and **decomposition**.

Key truths:

> 1. *Time is not a barrier.* Lazarus had been dead four days, yet Jesus restored him fully.
> 2. *Life is in His command.* John 1:4 says, "In Him was life." Dominion over matter includes dominion over life itself.
> 3. *Foretaste of ultimate restoration:* This miracle previews the resurrection of Christ and of all creation.

Christological Biblical Promises About Possessing the Earth

The Biblical Promises explored in chapter four locate God's intentions for the patriarchs, however, there are promises made through Christ who was there in the beginning (John 1:1) that further support the promise of inheritance.

1. *"Blessed are the meek, for they shall inherit the earth."* (Matthew 5:5 / Psalm 37:11)

Jesus pronounces a radical reversal of worldly values: "the meek" (those marked by strength under control) will inherit the earth (Reddit). In Old Testament imagery, inheriting the land pointed to both physical territory and spiritual favor. In the Sermon on the Mount, Jesus aligns meekness with Kingdom citizenship, not weakness, but rather humility coupled with faith in God's justice.

In Psalm 37, the psalmist repeats and expands on this promise: "the meek shall inherit the land and delight themselves in abundant peace" (Darkened Glass Reflections). The context is vital: while the wicked seem to prosper, the humble and trusting find lasting rest and divine vindication. This promise speaks against aggression and striving; it assures that true dominion comes through surrendered strength.

For believers today, this beatitude is a call to internalize meekness, not inaction, but deep trust in God's timing and purpose. When aggression and self-promotion dominate our world, meekness positions us to receive God's lasting presence, peace, and authority, the real "inheritance of earth." It's a spiritual posture that summons Kingdom reward, not entitlement.

2. *"Ask of Me, and I will give You the nations for Your inheritance, and the ends of the earth for Your possession." (Psalm 2:8)*

Here, God invites the King (ultimately Christ) to ask for dominion, promising *"the nations... the ends of the earth"* as heritage (NIV Bible, bibleref.com). This divine call to ask is crucial; it implies intentionality and relational intimacy, not passive inheritance. The psalm envisions a global Kingdom that expands through right request and right Sonship.

In Christian interpretation, Psalm 2 is fulfilled in Jesus and, by extension, in those who share His identity. As co-heirs with Christ (Romans 8:17), believers are invited into this inheritance of global dominion, not through conquest, but through covenant relationship, intercession, and alignment with the Father's heart.

Practically, this promise energizes our spiritual imagination. It encourages believers to pray expectantly for nations, to see every sphere of society as "our inheritance," and to steward the earth with authority born not of ambition, but of Father-son relationship. Dominion becomes an expression of worship and intercession, not politics alone.

3. "For the promise that he would be heir of the world was not to Abraham or to his seed through the law, but through the righteousness of faith." (Romans 4:13)

Paul reflects on God's promise to Abraham, clarifying that his inheritance of the world was not through legal merit, but through faith in the God who justifies (CGG). Abraham's belief made him a recipient of global blessing, not limited to land, but extended to all creation. His faith unlocked Covenant expansion beyond geographic borders.

This promise transcends generations: all who live by faith are counted into Abraham's lineage, becoming heirs of world: a spiritual, cosmic inheritance that includes participation in God's redemptive rule over creation. Because of Jesus, inherited promise is not only ethnic or territorial; it is cosmic and covenantal.

For us, Romans 4:13 reframes inheritance not as something earned but received by believing alignment with God's way. It invites believers to exercise faith that touches all dimensions of influence, cultural, environmental, economic, as heirs of the world empowered by God's righteousness, not by human striving.

Summary Table

Promise	Key Passage	Summary
Meek inheriting the earth	Matthew 5:5; Psalm 37:11	Humility and trust lead to lasting spiritual and material inheritance.
Nations as inheritance	Psalm 2:8	Believers can ask and steward global dominion through Kingdom intimacy and intercession.
Heir of the world through faith	Romans 4:13	Faith connects us to Abraham's promise - possession of the world through covenant, not law.

These promises, rooted in humility, faith, and divine invitation, converge: They call Christians to live with authority, stewardship, and expectation not as rulers by force, but as children of the King destined to bring heaven's rule to earth.

Why This Matters for Us Today

Neither Jesus' promises nor miracles were ancient oath or wonders of yesterday. His covenants stand and His miracles are **templates for the believer's authority.** He told His disciples:

> "Truly, truly, I say to you, whoever believes in me will also do the works that I do; and greater works than these will he do..." (John 14:12 ESV)

This means:
- We are called to **speak to storms,** literal and figurative, in our environments.
- We can **call** forth provision in times of scarcity.
- We are authorized to **heal** through prayer and Spirit-empowered action.
- We must engage in the **restoration of creation,** from environmental stewardship to scientific innovation, in alignment with the Creator's will.

Conclusion: The Pattern of the King

Jesus did not just come to save souls; He came to **model rulership over the material world**. Every miracle was an act of governance; the King exercising authority in the physical realm. In Him, we see the Genesis Mandate fully expressed: the image and likeness of God bringing the earth into alignment with heaven's will.

If we are to be His disciples in truth, we must not only preach His words but also walk in His works. We do this by stewarding creation, solving material problems, and demonstrating to a watching world that **the King still commands creation.**

Chapter 6

ୋ

As He Is, So Are We

The Foundation of Identity

The Apostle John gives one of the most staggering identity statements in all of Scripture when he writes, *"As He is, so are we in this world."* (1 John 4:17) He does not say as He was, looking back to a historical Jesus walking in Galilee, nor does he say as He will be in His future glory. He speaks in the present tense: **as He is right now in heavenly majesty, so are we in this world right now.** This is not poetic exaggeration. This is divine revelation, and it must become the foundation of how we see ourselves.

This verse forces us to reframe everything we believe about our role in the material world. Jesus is seated at the right hand of the Father, reigning over all creation, with every power and principality under His feet (Ephesians 1:20–22). If *"as He is, so are we"* is true, as we know it to be, then our identity is not defined by human frailty, but by His authority. This truth shatters the powerless mentality the church has too often adopted and replaces it with a kingdom consciousness that expects to rule, subdue, and govern the physical order.

Jesus as the Model of Dominion

Jesus did not merely preach about the Kingdom of God, He demonstrated it. Every miracle was a visible manifestation of His authority over the material world. When He turned water into wine (John 2:1–11), He exercised command over chemical processes. When He multiplied loaves and fish (Matthew 14:13–21), He bypassed natural laws of food production. When He walked on water (Matthew 14:25) and calmed the storm (Mark 4:39), He exerted mastery over gravitational forces, wind currents, and wave dynamics.

In all these acts, Jesus was not showing off His divinity alone. He was modeling what a human walking in perfect alignment with the Father could do. This is why He could say without hesitation, *"The works that I do you will do also; and greater works than these shall you do, because I go to My Father."* (John 14:12) He was handing the template of dominion to His followers, fully expecting them to continue the work.

We Are Authorized to Continue His Works

Jesus' miracles were a revelation of the Genesis Mandate in living color. As discussed, in Genesis 1:26-28, God gave man dominion over the earth, its creatures, and its resources. Sin temporarily disrupted that dominion, but in Christ, it is restored. This is why Jesus didn't simply rescue us from hell. He also reinstated our original position as stewards and governors of creation.

The early disciples understood this. Peter's shadow healed the sick (Acts 5:15-16). Philip was supernaturally transported from one location to another (Acts 8:39-40). Paul shook a deadly viper into the fire without harm (Acts 28:3-6) and healed multitudes through handkerchiefs and aprons that touched his body (Acts 19:11-12). These were not isolated spectacles, they were the continuation of Jesus' ministry through His body on earth: us.

Creation Groaning for the Sons of God

Paul writes in Romans 8:19-22,

> *"For the creation waits with eager longing for the revealing of the sons of God. For the creation was subjected to futility, not willingly, but because of Him who subjected it, in hope that the creation itself will be set free from its bondage to corruption and obtain the freedom of the*

glory of the children of God. For we know that the whole creation has been groaning together in the pains of childbirth until now."

This is a cosmic statement. Creation, the material order of the universe, is personified as longing for humanity to step back into its rightful role. The earth, seas, skies, and all resources are groaning under the weight of misuse, exploitation, and neglect. They are waiting for the sons and daughters of God to manifest the wisdom, authority, and stewardship of Christ in the physical world. When we operate in our restored dominion, we don't just benefit ourselves, but bring liberation to the entire created order.

This means environmental decay, resource mismanagement, and societal collapse are not merely political or economic issues. They are the direct result of absent sons and daughters who have not stepped into their rulership. The groaning of creation is a summons to rise.

Scientific Parallels to Our Dominion

Science, far from contradicting Scripture, often confirms what the Word has been declaring for millennia. Modern physics reveals that the universe is held together by unseen forces and invisible particles. Hebrews 11:3 affirms this: *"By faith we understand that the worlds were framed by the word of God, so that the things which are seen were not made of things which are visible."* Quantum mechanics now tells us that every atom is a collection of subatomic particles held together by precise laws; laws that are responsive to sound, energy, and frequency.

When Jesus spoke to storms, multiplied matter, or altered physical states, He was engaging with the elemental structure of creation. He was demonstrating mastery at the subatomic level; a level we are now rediscovering scientifically. Studies on sound frequencies show that vibrations can alter the structure of matter, heal biological tissue, and even break down solid objects. This aligns perfectly with biblical accounts of walls collapsing at Jericho through sound, or prophetic declarations bringing physical change.

If *"As He is, so are we,"* then we, too, have the capacity, under divine direction, to influence the material world in ways that science is only beginning to understand. The key is alignment with the Father's will, not random experimentation.

The Practical Outworking of "As He Is"

To live "As He is" requires more than mental agreement. It requires intentional cultivation of faith, obedience, and spiritual discipline. We must **first** renew our minds to accept the reality of our authority. Too many believers cancel their own dominion with words of limitation, saying, "I can't" or "That's impossible." Jesus never spoke like that, and neither should we.

Second, we must learn to hear and act on the Father's instructions. Jesus said, "The Son can do nothing of Himself, but what He sees the Father do" (John 5:19). Dominion is not about reckless displays of power; it is about executing heaven's agenda on earth. That requires intimacy with God.

Third, we must be willing to step out in faith and act. Peter only walked on water because he stepped out of the boat. We will never know the extent of our authority if we remain in the safety of theory. Action is the proving ground of dominion.

The Expectation of Greater Works

Jesus promised greater works (John 14:12) which is not limited to greater in magnitude, but also in scope and reach. Through technology, communication, and global travel, the body of Christ today has opportunities to influence the material world on a scale unimaginable in the first century. This includes harnessing renewable resources, advancing medical breakthroughs, reforming corrupt systems, and stewarding the planet in a way that reflects the King's heart.

The greater works are not just spiritual conversions,

but the transformation of the physical world to reflect the order and abundance of heaven. The sons and daughters of God must take their place in every field, science, politics, economics, arts, and agriculture, and manifest the rulership of Christ.

Our Call to Manifestation
The statement *"As He is, so are we in this world"* is both a description and a mandate. It tells us who we are and what we must do. The material world is not neutral ground, it is territory awaiting governance. Whether it is a storm threatening a city, a scarcity of resources, or the exploitation of land, the question remains: will the sons and daughters of God rise to rule as He rules?

Creation is waiting. Heaven is watching. The King has already shown us the way. Now, it is time to walk as He walked, speak as He spoke, and govern as He governs, for as He is, so are we in this world.

A Closer Look at The Apostolic Demonstration of Shared Dominion
The ministry of the apostles is living proof that the dominion Jesus exercised over the material world was not exclusive to Him. After His ascension, His followers stepped into the same authority and continued His works with striking

similarity. This was not a diluted version of His power but the same Spirit working through them, confirming His own words: *"He who believes in Me, the works that I do he will do also."* (John 14:12)

Peter, for example, demonstrated mastery over the material and physical world repeatedly. In Acts 3:6–8, he spoke to a man lame from birth, commanding, "In the name of Jesus Christ of Nazareth, rise up and walk." Instantly, the man's body responded to that authority, bypassing years of muscular atrophy and neurological disuse. Later, even Peter's shadow carried healing virtue (Acts 5:15–16) which suggests a tangible manifestation of dominion over the physical environment much like the woman who touched the hem of Jesus' garment and was healed.

Paul's ministry further confirms this principle. Acts 19:11–12 records that God worked unusual miracles by his hands, so that even cloths from his body carried healing power to the sick and delivered the demonized. In Acts 28:3–6, he survived a venomous viper bite with no harm, displaying mastery over the biological effects of poison. And in Acts 20:9–12, he raised Eutychus from the dead after a fatal fall; a miracle echoing Jesus' own resurrections. Philip's supernatural transportation in Acts 8:39–40 is another striking example. After baptizing the Ethiopian eunuch, the Spirit of the Lord physically carried him to

Azotus. This demonstrates dominion over spatial location and matter, showing that the miraculous was not limited to healings, but extended into realms of time, space, and movement.

These apostolic accounts are not given as historical curiosities but as precedent-setting examples. They confirm that the works of Jesus were intended to be replicated by His body, the Church. The same Spirit that raised Christ from the dead dwells in us (Romans 8:11), empowering us to walk as He walked. The ministry of the apostles reveals that the declaration *"As He is, so are we"* was never meant to be a poetic metaphor but a functional reality in the life of every believer.

Chapter 7

ଓଃ

Historical and Modern Examples of Possessing the Earth by Faith

The promises of possession are not merely theological abstractions. They have been lived out by real men and women throughout history. These individuals combined deep spiritual convictions with remarkable achievements in science, governance, business, and culture. Their stories prove that it is possible to walk in the authority of God's promises and shape the material world for His glory.

George Washington Carver – Turning Peanuts into Prosperity

George Washington Carver (1864–1943), born into slavery, rose to become one of America's most celebrated scientists and agricultural innovators. Carver's groundbreaking work with peanuts, sweet potatoes, and crop rotation revolutionized Southern agriculture, restoring depleted soil and bringing economic renewal to struggling farmers. Carver was unashamedly a man of prayer. He famously said, "God is going to reveal to us things He never revealed before if we put our hands in His." His laboratory was not just a place of experimentation, but a sanctuary where he sought divine wisdom for practical problems. In many ways, Carver exemplified Genesis 1:28. He exercised dominion over the earth's resources and using that mastery to bless others.

C.S. Lewis – Ruling in the Realm of Ideas

While possession often refers to material territory, influence over the realm of thought is equally significant. C.S. Lewis (1898–1963) was an Oxford professor, literary scholar, and one of the 20th century's greatest Christian apologists. Through works like *Mere Christianity*, *The Screwtape Letters*, and *The Chronicles of Narnia*, Lewis shaped the imagination and theology of millions.

His writing defended the faith with intellectual rigor while presenting Christian truth in ways that captivated both believers and skeptics. This is possession in the arena of culture, not seizing land, but seizing minds, hearts, and imaginations; advancing the Kingdom through literature and ideas.

Katherine Johnson – Calculating Humanity's Reach into the Heavens

Katherine Johnson (1918–2020), an African-American mathematician and devout Christian, was instrumental in NASA's space program. Her precise calculations enabled John Glenn's orbital flight and the Apollo 11 moon landing.

Johnson saw her work as part of a divine calling, using her God-given intellect to expand humanity's reach. In doing so, she demonstrated Psalm 115:16 that says, *"The highest heavens belong to the Lord, but the earth He has given to mankind."* She proved that believers can influence even the most advanced realms of science and exploration.

William Wilberforce – Legislating Freedom

William Wilberforce (1759–1833) was a British parliamentarian whose Christian convictions drove him to lead the abolition of the Transatlantic Slave Trade. For over two decades, he fought political opposition, personal illness, and social resistance until the Slavery Abolition Act was passed in 1833, just days before his death.

Wilberforce's story demonstrates possession in governance. He understood that inheriting the earth includes shaping its laws, protecting its people, and dismantling systems of oppression. His life fulfills Proverbs 29:2 that says,

"When the righteous are in authority, the people rejoice."

R.G. LeTourneau – Kingdom Industry

R.G. LeTourneau (1888–1969) was an industrialist and inventor of massive earth-moving machines. Known as "God's businessman," he committed 90% of his income to Kingdom work and lived on the remaining 10%.

LeTourneau's innovations transformed construction, mining, and infrastructure projects worldwide. His story shows that business can be a platform for possession, where technological creativity is coupled with radical generosity to fund Kingdom initiatives.

Mother Teresa – Possessing the Streets of Calcutta

Though she owned no land or amassed great wealth, Mother Teresa (1910–1997) possessed a moral and spiritual authority that commanded global attention. Her ministry to the poorest of the poor in Calcutta demonstrated that possession is not only about material resources but about occupying spaces of suffering with the presence of Christ. She changed the conversation about human dignity, influencing nations, leaders, and institutions to care for the marginalized; a testament to Isaiah 58's promise that those who serve the needy will "be called repairer of broken walls, restorer of streets with dwellings."

Elon Musk – Innovation with Moral Conversations

While Elon Musk is not known for orthodox Christian faith, he often engages with moral questions about humanity's future and stewardship of the earth. Believers can take note of his example in innovation by pushing the boundaries of energy, space, and transportation, but apply it with a Kingdom lens. When coupled with spiritual convictions, such innovation becomes not just technological achievement but divine stewardship.

Why These Examples Matter

These lives teach us that the possession mandate is not limited to preachers or missionaries. Whether in laboratories, courtrooms, factories, boardrooms, or mission fields, God raises up His people to occupy areas of influence and shape the future of the world.

The consistent thread is **faithful stewardship of gifts**, be it intellectual brilliance, creative vision, moral courage, or industrial skill. These individuals embodied Romans 8:19 by manifesting their sonship in tangible, world-changing ways.

Chapter 8

☙

Promises of Possession: God's Covenant for His People to Inherit the Earth

The idea that God intends His people to possess the earth is not a minor theme in Scripture, it is a core part of the covenant story. From Genesis to Revelation, God ties His blessing to inheritance, rulership, and the occupation of tangible territory. These promises are not merely spiritual metaphors; they carry practical, physical, and material implications for how believers should live in the world today. Sadly, for much of church history, this truth has been underemphasized or spiritualized to the point of irrelevance. Yet the Word of God is unmistakable: the Creator never designed His children to live as tenants in the world, but as heirs and stewards of His creation. In this chapter, we will explore the biblical promises of possession, examine how they are fulfilled in Christ, and see how they apply to our lives in practical ways.

The Old Testament Foundations of Possession
The Promise to Abraham

One of the earliest and clearest promises of possession is found in God's covenant with Abraham. In Genesis 12:1–3, God calls Abraham out of his homeland and promises to give him land, make his name great, and bless all the families of the earth through him. Later, in Genesis 13:14–15, God says:

> *"Lift up your eyes from where you are and look north and south, east and west. All the land that you see I will give to you and your offspring forever."*

This was not a symbolic promise, it was about real land, measurable territory, and tangible resources. The land represented God's generosity and the covenantal inheritance of Abraham's descendants.

For believers today, Galatians 3:29 affirms that "If you belong to Christ, then you are Abraham's seed, and heirs according to the promise." This means the promise of inheritance is directly connected to our identity in Christ. We are not spiritual squatters, we are covenant heirs destined to steward what God places under our authority.

The Inheritance of Israel

The conquest of Canaan under Joshua was a physical manifestation of God's promise to Abraham. God did not merely deliver Israel from Egypt, He brought them into a land flowing with milk and honey (Deuteronomy 6:10–12). Over and over, the Lord reminded them that the land was a gift, but they were to possess it actively.

Possession required action. Israel had to fight battles, drive out hostile nations, and establish godly governance. This principle remains true today: inheritance must be claimed and maintained. Spiritual passivity will not bring the fullness of God's promises into our lives.

Psalm 37:29 reinforces this truth:

"The righteous will inherit the land and dwell in it forever." This is both a statement of divine intent and a call to stewardship. God wants His people to be settled, secure, and influential in the earth, not transient wanderers without a stake in the material world.

New Testament Continuation

The New Testament does not abolish the idea of possessing the earth. It expands it. Jesus declares in Matthew 5:5:

> *"Blessed are the meek, for they shall inherit the earth."*

Meekness is not weakness; it is disciplined strength

under God's authority. It is the posture of a ruler who governs with humility, but walks in undeniable authority. Christ did not say His followers would inherit heaven alone. He explicitly said the earth.

Paul affirms in Romans 4:13 that Abraham's promise was "that he would be heir of the world." Notice the language: the world, not just a patch of land in Canaan. Through Christ, the scope of the promise widens to include global influence, cross-cultural expansion, and the stewardship of resources across the nations.

Twelve Key Scriptures on Possession
To build a solid biblical foundation, here are twelve passages that confirm God's intention for His people to possess the earth.

1. Genesis 1:28 – *"Be fruitful and multiply, fill the earth and subdue it. Have dominion…"*
God's first words to humanity were about rulership. This was a mandate to actively manage the resources of the material world. Dominion means mastery over agriculture, industry, technology, and culture. It was never revoked, it was reaffirmed in Christ.

2. Psalm 2:8 – *"Ask of Me, and I will give You the nations for Your inheritance, and the ends of the earth for Your possession."*

This messianic promise applies to Christ and, by extension, to His Body. Nations are not just geographical entities but centers of culture, governance, and economy. Possession here means influence and governance over the systems that shape the world.

3. Deuteronomy 28:1-2 – *"The Lord your God will set you high above all nations… and all these blessings will come upon you."*

Height in biblical language speaks of influence and prominence. God intends for His people to operate from the top, not in arrogance, but in order to bless and shape the world according to Kingdom values.

4. Isaiah 60:5 – *"The wealth of the nations shall come to you."*

This verse ties possession directly to the transfer of resources. Economic dominion is part of the inheritance package, allowing God's people to fund righteous causes and dismantle systems of oppression.

5. Proverbs 13:22 – *"The wealth of the sinner is laid up for the righteous."*

This promise reveals that economic power

is not inherently tied to unrighteousness. In God's timing, resources will be transferred to those who will steward them according to His purposes.

6. Matthew 16:19 – *"I will give you the keys of the kingdom of heaven…"*

Keys represent authority and access. To possess the earth, believers must operate with the keys of revelation, strategy, and supernatural favor.

7. Romans 8:17 – *"If we are children, then we are heirs — heirs of God and co-heirs with Christ."*

As co-heirs, we share in Christ's inheritance, which includes authority over all creation (Colossians 1:16).

8. 1 Corinthians 3:21-23 – *"All things are yours… the world, or life, or death, or the present or the future — all are yours, and you are Christ's, and Christ is God's."*

Paul's declaration is destiny-altering. All things are ours in Christ. This leaves no room for a theology of lack.

9. Psalm 115:16 – *"The highest heavens belong to the Lord, but the earth He has given to man-*

kind."

Ownership of the earth has been delegated. It is not God's will for us to surrender it to systems of darkness.

10. Revelation 5:10 – *"You have made them to be a kingdom and priests… and they will reign on the earth."*

The future is not about escaping the earth but reigning on it under Christ's eternal governance.

11. Joshua 1:3 – *"Every place that the sole of your foot will tread upon I have given you."*

Possession requires action. We must walk, build, and establish presence where God leads us.

12. Isaiah 61:6 – *"You will feed on the wealth of nations, and in their riches you will boast."*

This is not a license for greed but a prophetic vision of provision and empowerment for Kingdom purposes.

The Creation is Waiting for Us

Romans 8:19–22 is a powerful reminder:

> *"For the creation waits in eager expectation for the children of God to be revealed… that the*

creation itself will be liberated from its bondage to decay and brought into the freedom and glory of the children of God."

This means that the earth itself, its resources, systems, and ecosystems, is waiting for righteous rulers to manifest. Creation is groaning under mismanagement, corruption, and exploitation. As sons of God, we are called to bring restoration, healing, and righteous governance to the material world.

Possession in Our Time

To *"possess the earth"* today may not always mean military conquest or literal land seizure. It can mean acquiring businesses, influencing legislation, controlling supply chains, and innovating in science and technology with Kingdom values at the core. It can mean reclaiming arts, media, and education from destructive narratives and restoring them to truth and beauty.

Possession in our generation requires three things:
- **Faith** - the unshakable belief that God has given us authority.
- **Obedience** - the willingness to act in alignment with His commands.
- **Stewardship** - the skill to manage resources for long-term Kingdom impact.

The promises of possession are not relics of ancient history. They are the present inheritance of every believer in Christ. From Abraham's covenant to Jesus' Beatitudes, from Joshua's conquest to the apostles' expansion, the message is clear: God's people are meant to occupy, influence, and steward the earth until the return of the King.

To deny or ignore these promises is to live beneath our calling. To embrace them is to step into the role for which we were created: rulers of the material world, heirs of the earth, and stewards of the Creator's masterpiece.

Chapter 9
ଔ
The War of Worlds: Atrocities for Possession of Land and Wealth

From Genesis to modern times, the struggle for dominion over the material world has not been an abstract theological concept. It has been a brutal, bloody reality. Nations have risen and fallen on the back of wars waged to claim land, minerals, ports, oil fields, rivers, and mountains. In nearly every case, the victors have justified their conquest as necessary for "civilization," "progress," or "security," but history unmasks the darker motive: the insatiable human drive to possess the wealth of the nations. Scripture speaks of this drive, warning of kings who "devour widows' houses" (Luke 20:47) and of empires that plunder the resources of others (Habakkuk 2:6–9). This chapter will examine ten pivotal examples, showing how each reflects the global battle for territory and wealth, and why God's people must understand this war in order to walk in righteous dominion.

1. The Conquest of the Americas & Native American Displacement

The Event (Historical Facts)

In 1492, Christopher Columbus's arrival in the Caribbean set in motion a chain of events that would forever alter the Americas. Over the next 400 years, Spanish, Portuguese, French, Dutch, and English colonizers swept across the continents, bringing advanced weaponry, new diseases, and an imperial hunger for land. Entire civilizations, the Aztec, Inca, and countless indigenous nations, were decimated. By the 19th century, the U.S. had driven Native American tribes westward under policies like the Indian Removal Act of 1830, culminating in tragedies such as the Trail of Tears.

The Land and Wealth Factor

This was not merely about new homes for settlers. It was about gold in the rivers, fertile soil for agriculture, control over trade routes, and access to forests, fisheries, and later oil reserves. Colonizers understood that whoever owned the land controlled the economy and the future.

The Spiritual/Biblical Connection

The Bible warns against moving ancient boundary stones

(Deuteronomy 19:14) and condemns nations that seize land through violence. The conquest of the Americas is a textbook example of violating God's principles for just dominion. Instead of stewardship, it was theft under the guise of destiny.

Modern Lessons and Ongoing Struggles
Today, Native American reservations sit on some of the poorest lands, yet many contain valuable minerals now coveted by corporations. The spirit that drove European conquest still operates; one that sees land as loot rather than as sacred trust. Believers must discern the difference between righteous possession and exploitative acquisition.

2. The Transatlantic Slave Trade & Colonial Resource Plunder
The Event (Historical Facts)
From the 16th to the 19th century, over 12 million Africans were captured, sold, and shipped across the Atlantic, primarily to the Americas. This human trafficking was not only a moral atrocity, but also an economic system that built the wealth of European powers and their colonies. The labor of enslaved people was used to extract sugar, cotton, tobacco, and other resources, feeding the industrial rise of the West.

The Land and Wealth Factor
Plantations in the Caribbean and the American South became some of the most profitable enterprises in the world. The wealth generated was not simply in crops, it was in the ownership of human beings as property, reducing God's image-bearers to tools for extracting wealth from the land.

The Spiritual/Biblical Connection
Scripture teaches that "the laborer is worthy of his wages" (Luke 10:7) and condemns the kidnapping of people (Exodus 21:16). The Transatlantic Slave Trade was a twofold crime: stealing both people and the fruits of their labor.

Modern Lessons and Ongoing Struggles
Though slavery is officially abolished, modern equivalents exist in sweatshops, forced labor, and economic systems designed to keep certain populations landless and powerless. The struggle for reparations and land return is not merely political. It's a spiritual battle for justice and restoration.

3. The Scramble for Africa
The Event (Historical Facts)
Between 1884 and 1885, European powers gathered at the Berlin Conference to divide the countries of the African continent among themselves without a single African representative present. The colonial carve-up ignored ethnic

boundaries, resource stewardship, and native sovereignty.

The Land and Wealth Factor
Africa's gold, diamonds, ivory, and fertile lands were the true prizes. Colonizers built railways and ports, not for African development, but to facilitate the export of raw materials to Europe.

The Spiritual/Biblical Connection
Habakkuk 2:12 warns: *"Woe to him who builds a town with blood and founds a city on iniquity!"* The Scramble for Africa was literally built on blood and iniquity, reflecting the same spirit that Babylon carried in Scripture, a system built on exploitation.

Modern Lessons and Ongoing Struggles
Even post-independence, many African nations remain trapped in neo-colonial trade agreements and debt structures that continue to siphon resources to former colonial masters. Dominion without justice is simply theft with a crown.

4. The British Colonization of India
The Event (Historical Facts)
The British East India Company gradually took control of India in the 18th century, later replaced by direct British Crown rule. Through military force, economic manipulation, and legal control, Britain dominated India for nearly

200 years.

The Land and Wealth Factor
India was not just a source of spices. It was the "jewel in the crown" of the British Empire because of its cotton, tea, opium, and vast agricultural lands. The British drained India's wealth, causing famines and impoverishment.

The Spiritual/Biblical Connection
Isaiah 10:13 speaks of arrogant rulers who say, "By the strength of my hand I have done it… and I have robbed their treasures." The British imperial attitude mirrors this biblical condemnation.

Modern Lessons and Ongoing Struggles
Today, India is reclaiming its global economic place, but the wounds of colonial extraction still influence trade, infrastructure, and social divides. The call for believers is to engage in nation-building that restores dignity and sovereignty.

5. The Armenian Genocide (1915–1917)
The Event (Historical Facts)
During World War I, the Ottoman Empire systematically deported and massacred an estimated 1.5 million Armenians. While ethnic and religious motives were present, economic motives ran just as deep. Armenian businesses, farms, and properties were confiscated, enriching those

loyal to the Ottoman regime. Entire villages were emptied, and their lands redistributed.

The Land and Wealth Factor
The genocide cleared the way for the Ottoman state and allied groups to seize valuable farmlands, trade routes, and urban properties. The strategic location of Armenia's lands meant control over mountain passes, fertile valleys, and regional commerce.

The Spiritual/Biblical Connection
Micah 2:1–2 warns of those "who covet fields and seize them… who oppress a man and his house." The Armenian genocide fits this biblical indictment perfectly: murder as a tool for land acquisition.

Modern Lessons and Ongoing Struggles
Even today, Armenian-Turkish relations are strained and historical denial is often linked to the unwillingness to address stolen property and land. Without repentance and restitution, nations cannot break free from the curse of unjust gain.

6. The Nazi Expansion & the Holocaust
The Event (Historical Facts)
Adolf Hitler's Third Reich didn't only seek to eliminate Jews and other targeted groups, it aimed to establish Lebensraum or "living space" for the Aryan race. This meant

conquering Eastern Europe, displacing its inhabitants, and seizing property, factories, and farmland.

The Land and Wealth Factor
The Holocaust was intertwined with mass theft. Jewish-owned businesses, homes, art collections, and bank accounts were confiscated. Entire regions were depopulated so that German settlers could move in and exploit the agricultural and industrial capacity.

The Spiritual/Biblical Connection
Proverbs 22:28 warns, "Do not move the ancient boundary that your fathers have set." Nazi ideology did precisely that in obliterating borders, identities, and inheritances for the sake of imperial control.

Modern Lessons and Ongoing Struggles
Post-war restitution efforts recovered some assets, but much stolen wealth remains hidden or unreturned. This underscores that wars for land are almost always wars for concentrated wealth.

7. The Apartheid Land Seizures in South Africa
The Event (Historical Facts)
Under apartheid (1948–1994), South Africa's white minority government enacted laws that removed Black South Africans from their ancestral lands, confining them to "homelands" while prime agricultural and mineral-rich

lands were claimed by white settlers.

The Land and Wealth Factor
South Africa's gold and diamond mines, some of the richest in the world, became the backbone of its economy, yet Black South Africans, who historically inhabited these regions, were excluded from ownership and wealth benefits.

The Spiritual/Biblical Connection
Ezekiel 45:9 commands, "Put away violence and oppression, and do what is just and right. Stop dispossessing my people." Apartheid was the antithesis of this divine command, institutionalizing dispossession.

Modern Lessons and Ongoing Struggles
Land reform remains one of South Africa's most divisive political issues. Until land ownership reflects justice, the spiritual and economic wounds of apartheid will linger.

8. The Displacement of the Palestinians (1948–Present)

The Event (Historical Facts)
Following the creation of the State of Israel in 1948, hundreds of thousands of Palestinians were displaced from their homes and lands during the Arab-Israeli conflict. This displacement, known as the Nakba ("catastrophe"), has led to decades of conflict, refugee crises, and contested claims.

The Land and Wealth Factor
The issue is more than identity, it's also about fertile lands, water resources, and control over strategic locations. Land once tilled by Palestinian farmers was repurposed for new settlements and infrastructure.

The Spiritual/Biblical Connection
While Scripture affirms God's covenant with Israel regarding the land, it also commands the just treatment of the "stranger." (Leviticus 19:34) Dominion must never disregard God's justice for all peoples.

Modern Lessons and Ongoing Struggles
The unresolved land issue fuels one of the world's longest-standing conflicts. Any lasting peace will require a righteous approach to land and property rights.

9. The Japanese Occupation of Korea (1910–1945)
The Event (Historical Facts)
Japan annexed Korea in 1910, imposing cultural assimilation, forced labor, and resource extraction. Korean lands were seized for Japanese settlers and companies, while native Koreans were heavily taxed and pushed off fertile lands.

The Land and Wealth Factor
Japan's interest in Korea was rooted in strategic geography and resources of coal, iron, and agricultural produce. Land

reform favored Japanese landowners, concentrating wealth and control.

The Spiritual/Biblical Connection
Isaiah 5:8 warns, "Woe to those who join house to house, who add field to field, until there is no more room." The Japanese expansion exemplifies this prophetic warning.

Modern Lessons and Ongoing Struggles
Even decades after liberation, economic disparities and historical grievances shape Korean-Japanese relations, reminding us that stolen land leaves generational scars.

10. The Forced Relocations for the Three Gorges Dam in China

The Event (Historical Facts)
In the late 20th and early 21st centuries, China constructed the massive Three Gorges Dam, the world's largest hydroelectric project. While it brought energy benefits, it displaced over 1.2 million people, flooding towns, farmland, and cultural heritage sites.

The Land and Wealth Factor
The displacement was not for foreign conquest but for domestic economic gain: electricity, water control, and industrial expansion. Yet the human cost was immense, with many relocated to less fertile lands.

The Spiritual/Biblical Connection

Proverbs 29:2 declares, *"When the righteous are in authority, the people rejoice; but when the wicked rule, the people groan."* The groaning of those displaced without fair compensation mirrors this truth.

Modern Lessons and Ongoing Struggles

Development without justice mirrors conquest without morality. Kingdom-minded dominion must always balance stewardship of resources with the dignity of the people who inhabit the land.

The Battle for the Earth Is a Spiritual War Over Possession From the Garden of Eden to the pages of Revelation, Scripture presents the earth not as an abstract spiritual symbol, but as tangible real estate entrusted to humanity under God's authority. Psalm 24:1 declares, *"The earth is the LORD's and the fullness thereof, the world and those who dwell therein."* Yet from Cain's murder of Abel to modern geopolitics, the human story reveals that unrighteous men and empires continually attempt to seize what God owns, often at the cost of human life.

Every atrocity in this chapter, from the displacement of Native Americans to the genocides of the 21st century, shares a common thread: the belief that dominion is a human right to be pursued at all costs, even if it means violence, theft, and oppression. This is the counterfeit version of God's mandate. Whereas God's dominion order involves stewardship, justice, and blessing for all nations (Genesis 1:28; Psalm 72:8–17), the world's dominion order operates on greed, exploitation, and the enrichment of the few.

The Cosmic Context of the Land Struggle

The biblical narrative shows that the battle for the earth is not merely political or economic, it is spiritual. Satan himself claimed ownership of the kingdoms of the world when tempting Jesus in Luke 4:5–7, offering Him "all their authority and splendor" if He would bow down and worship. The implication is staggering: fallen powers actively contest God's people for control of the material world. This is why Paul calls Satan "the god of this world" (2 Corinthians 4:4), not because he has rightful title, but because he holds it through deception, violence, and sin.

When nations commit atrocities for land and wealth, they echo the serpent's ambition: to claim the earth apart from God's rule. This is why the quest for possession must be rooted in God's covenant purposes, not in the strategies of empire.

God's People Are Called to Possess Righteously

Jesus did not reject the concept of land, resources, or material dominion. He redefined how it is attained. "Blessed are the meek, for they shall inherit the earth" (Matthew 5:5). The meek are not the passive, but those submitted to God's will in their stewardship of the earth. Abraham's example is instructive: he refused to take spoils from the King of Sodom so that no one could claim they made him rich (Genesis 14:22–23). Dominion must come by divine grant, not by bloodshed and unrighteous acquisition.

As the heirs of the kingdom, we are not called to retreat from the material world but to inherit it (Romans 4:13). Yet our inheritance is not seized through conquest in the world's way, it is received through covenant faith, righteous labor, and the favor of God. Proverbs 13:22 tells us, "The wealth of the sinner is laid up for the just." This is a prophetic promise that the battle over the world's wealth will ultimately end in God's people possessing it for His purposes.

A Final Word on the Current Battle
The atrocities in history are reminders that the contest for the earth's resources is not over. Modern battles over land, oil, water rights, rare earth minerals, and strategic territory are simply the continuation of an ancient war. The church must awaken from its passive posture and recognize that possessing the earth is part of our divine mandate, not for exploitation, but for the expansion of God's justice, provi-

sion, and kingdom order.

If the righteous withdraw from this calling, unrighteous powers will continue to fill the vacuum. But if the sons and daughters of God rise, as Romans 8:19 declares, *"For the creation waits with eager longing for the revealing of the sons of God"* then the land, the seas, and all creation will see righteous dominion restored. The earth itself is groaning for this day (Romans 8:22), and it will come when God's people embrace both their spiritual and material inheritance.

Chapter 10
❧
Territorial Spirits and Why Believers Are Best Positioned to Defeat Them to Own Land Mass

The Invisible War Over Visible Land

The Bible presents the earth as a divinely allocated inheritance (Psalm 115:16). Yet Scripture also reveals that behind every earthly domain, nations, cities, and land masses, there are unseen rulers, *"spiritual forces of evil in the heavenly places"* (Ephesians 6:12). These are not abstract metaphors, they are territorial spirits, ancient beings assigned to regions who influence governments, economies, and cultures.

To claim land for God's kingdom, believers must understand that the battle is not only fought with legal documents and political negotiations, it is fought in the spiritual realm. This is why Jesus told us to "first bind the strong man" before taking his goods (Mark 3:27). Territorial spirits are "strong men" over geographical areas, and unless they are displaced spiritually, their grip on the land remains.

Biblical Evidence of Territorial Spirits
The Prince of Persia and Prince of Greece
Daniel 10 offers one of the clearest insights into territorial spirits. While fasting and praying for his people, Daniel receives a visitation from an angel who explains that his answer was delayed for twenty-one days because *"the prince of the kingdom of Persia withstood me."* (Daniel 10:13) This "prince" is not a human ruler, it is a spiritual being exercising authority over the Persian Empire. The angel adds that after dealing with this prince, the *"prince of Greece"* will come (Daniel 10:20).

Here, we see the pattern: great empires are not merely political, but are influenced by spiritual principalities. These beings resist the purposes of God for the land and its people. If Persia and Greece had spiritual rulers, then modern nations and cities are no different. Every region has spiritual strongholds, some rooted in idolatry, others in bloodshed, injustice, or covenant with darkness.

Gog, Magog, and Prophetic Territorial Control
In Ezekiel 38–39, we meet Gog of the land of Magog, a prophetic figure aligned with multiple nations against Israel.

Gog is more than a political leader, he is a territorial force orchestrating alliances to control strategic land. Revelation 20:8 shows Gog and Magog again, symbolizing global demonic opposition to God's reign in the earth's final chapter. The lesson here is that territorial spirits are not temporary. They persist across generations, influencing successive rulers and nations unless displaced by God's power.

Israel and Angelic Guardianship

Deuteronomy 32:8–9 (ESV) tells us: *"When the Most High gave to the nations their inheritance, when he divided mankind, he fixed the borders of the peoples according to the number of the sons of God. But the LORD's portion is his people, Jacob his allotted heritage."* This remarkable passage shows that in ancient times, God appointed spiritual beings ("sons of God") over different nations, but He Himself took Israel as His direct inheritance.

This means the concept of territorial spiritual authority is not just a demonic counterfeit, it was part of God's original administrative structure. The difference is that fallen beings now often occupy these positions illegitimately, using them to oppose God's plans.

The Devil as the Distributor of Fortunes

In Luke 4:5–7, Satan tempts Jesus by showing Him *"all the kingdoms of the world in a moment of time"* and says:

"To you I will give all this authority and their glory, for it has been delivered to me, and I give it to whom I will. If you, then, will worship me, it will all be yours."

The Greek word behind "devil" (*diabolos*) carries the idea of a slanderer, accuser, and divider, but here the function he claims is that of a **distributor of fortunes**. He presents himself as the one who can assign kingdoms and wealth. The tragedy is that much of the world still operates under this system. People, corporations, and governments bow to corrupt powers to gain access to land, resources, and influence.

Satan was not lying when he said the kingdoms were "delivered" to him. Adam's disobedience handed humanity's dominion over to the enemy (Genesis 3). Yet his offer to Jesus was a counterfeit shortcut. The real inheritance of the nations was promised to the Messiah by the Father (Psalm 2:8), and it would come through the cross, not compromise.

Believers' Power Over Demons - An Unshakable Reality

From the moment a believer is born again, they are transferred out of the kingdom of darkness into the kingdom of God's dear Son (Colossians 1:13). This is not a symbolic gesture. It is a legal and spiritual transaction that strips Satan of his authority over the child of God. Jesus Himself declared in **Luke 10:19**, *"Behold, I give you authority to trample on serpents and scorpions, and over all the power of the enemy, and nothing shall by any means hurt you."* This is not partial authority, it is total jurisdiction over demonic powers, whether they operate in the unseen realm or manifest through human agents.

Christ's victory at the cross was not a narrow escape, it was a public, crushing defeat of every demonic force. **Colossians 2:15** says, *"Having disarmed principalities and powers, He made a public spectacle of them, triumphing over them in it."* When Christ disarmed the enemy, He stripped him of every legal weapon. That same authority is now delegated to every believer. We are not negotiating with demons, we are enforcing the judgment already passed against them. To tolerate demonic harassment is to deny the legal right and power purchased by the blood of Jesus.

In **Mark 16:17**, Jesus made an unmistakable declaration: *"And these signs will follow those who believe: In My name they will cast out demons."* This is the believer's default setting, not an advanced spiritual level for a few elite Christians. The phrase "in My name" is a legal term. It means acting as Christ's representative with His full authority. When we command a demon to leave, we are not speaking in our own strength, we are speaking on behalf of the risen King whose throne is established above all principalities and powers. Demons know this authority. That is why in Acts 19:15, the evil spirit said to the impostors, *"Jesus I know, and Paul I know; but who are you?"* True believers are recognized and feared in the spiritual realm.

Furthermore, **1 John 4:4** declares, *"Greater is He who is in you than he who is in the world."* This is not poetic encouragement. It is a declaration of spiritual supremacy. The indwelling Holy Spirit is not intimidated by legions of demons, ancient curses, or territorial principalities. His power is infinite, His authority unquestionable, and His presence in the believer is the ultimate guarantee of victory. When the Spirit of God resides within us, no demon can stand its ground unless we allow it through ignorance or unbelief. This truth demands that we stop approaching demonic resistance with fear and instead confront it with the confidence of an authorized ambassador of Heaven.

Believers must understand: spiritual warfare is not about hoping to win. It is about enforcing an already-won victory. Satan's kingdom thrives only where ignorance, passivity, or disobedience reign. But when a Spirit-filled believer rises in the authority of the Word, armed with the name of Jesus and the power of the Holy Ghost, the demonic realm trembles. Our mandate is clear: *resist the devil, and he will flee* (James 4:7). Flee, not negotiate, not linger, not retaliate, but flee in terror. We are not victims of darkness, we are its conquerors. The believer is God's chosen instrument to evict, dismantle, and destroy the works of the devil wherever they are found.

Believers' Authority Over Territorial Spirits

The authority of the believer does not stop at casting out personal demons. It extends into the realm of territorial powers. These are the spiritual rulers that operate over cities, nations, and regions, influencing political climates, economic systems, and cultural patterns. Remember, **Daniel 10:13** reveals this reality when the angel sent to Daniel said, *"The prince of the kingdom of Persia withstood me twenty-one days."* This "prince" was no human. It was a demonic power assigned over Persia. These same dark forces still operate today, but the believer has authority to challenge and dislodge them because Jesus reigns *"far above all rule and authority and power and dominion."* (Ephesians 1:21) If Christ is above them, and we are seated with Him (Ephesians 2:6), then our authority is a shared authority over these entities.

When Satan tempted Jesus in **Luke 4:5–7**, he offered Him *"all the kingdoms of the world and their glory,"* claiming they had been delivered into his control and he could give them to whomever he chose. This was a direct confrontation over territorial dominion. But Christ rejected the compromise, choosing instead to take the kingdoms by conquest through His death, resurrection, and ascension. The point is clear: Satan still seeks to control land, nations, and the wealth they contain, but the believer, armed with Christ's victory, has the legal right to reclaim these territories for the Kingdom of God. This is not just a spiritual metaphor. Land, resources, and economies are part of the believer's inheritance in Christ (Psalm 2:8; Matthew 5:5).

Territorial spirits are often the invisible forces behind systemic poverty, perpetual wars, cultural corruption, and religious deception. They are the demonic administrators that distribute curses, confusion, and oppression over populations. But **Colossians 1:16–17** tells us that all thrones, dominions, principalities, and powers were created by Christ and for Christ and that He holds all things together. This means their existence is subject to His sovereignty, and through His Church, their assignments can be canceled. Believers, therefore, are not powerless bystanders but Heaven's authorized agents to break the grip of these spiritual overlords.

To deal with territorial spirits, the believer must step into **apostolic and prophetic prayer dimensions,** speaking to both the invisible and visible realms. **Jeremiah 1:10** gives the divine template: *"See, I have set you this day over nations and over kingdoms, to pluck up and to break down,* *to destroy and to overthrow, to build and to plant."* This is governmental language. Prayer at this level is not begging God to act, it is executing His decrees over cities and nations. The power to bind and loose (Matthew 18:18) applies not just to individuals but to spiritual climates and territorial strongholds.

Finally, believers must understand that the conquest of land and territories is a divine inheritance. **Psalm 24:1** declares, *"The earth is the Lord's, and the fullness thereof; the world, and they that dwell therein."* If the earth belongs to the Lord, and we are His heirs (Romans 8:17), then it follows that we are rightful co-owners and stewards. This makes our spiritual battle for land more than a matter of survival. It is about enforcing Heaven's title deed on the earth. Territorial spirits are trespassers, and as long as they remain unchallenged, they will control the wealth and destiny of nations. But the moment a believer rises in their authority and acts in alignment with Heaven, the grip of these powers begins to break, and the land begins to yield its strength to the Kingdom of God.

Why Believers Are Best Positioned to Defeat Territorial Spirits
We Have Legal Authority in Christ
Jesus declared in Matthew 28:18, *"All authority in heaven*

and on earth has been given to me." Because believers are in Christ, His authority is our authority (Luke 10:19). No territorial spirit can claim rightful ownership over land that the Lord has redeemed by His blood. While governments may pass laws, only the believer can claim spiritual title deed, enforcing God's will in prayer, prophetic declaration, and righteous action.

We Have the Indwelling Holy Spirit
Territorial spirits control through deception, fear, and spiritual blindness. But believers carry the Spirit of Truth (John 16:13), who exposes the enemy's schemes and guides us to victory. The Holy Spirit gives divine strategies for displacing spiritual powers just as God gave Joshua instructions to march around Jericho, or David insight on where to strike the Philistines.

We Operate From Heavenly Places
Ephesians 2:6 says God has *"raised us up with him and seated us with him in the heavenly places in Christ Jesus."* This means believers operate from a jurisdiction higher than that of any territorial spirit. From this position, we legislate in prayer, declare God's will, and command spiritual eviction notices over land, resources, and regions.

The Process of Defeating Territorial Spirits

Territorial spirits are not dislodged by accident. They are overthrown by deliberate spiritual strategy. Believers who wish to possess land, influence regions, or shift the atmosphere over cities must understand that they are stepping into a conflict that is as old as the Garden of Eden. Satan has always sought to dominate territory because whoever controls the land controls the destiny of the people on it. The Bible is clear: our weapons are not carnal but mighty through God to pull down strongholds (2 Corinthians 10:4). Below is a five-step process for breaking the grip of these regional powers and taking possession of the inheritance God has given.

1. Identification and Discernment of the Territorial Spirit

Before you can engage an enemy, you must know who or what you are dealing with. The first step is to discern the dominant spiritual power over the territory. This is what Daniel experienced in Daniel 10 when the angel spoke of being resisted by the "Prince of Persia" and later going to battle with the "Prince of Greece." These were not human rulers but high-ranking demonic beings assigned to control empires and resist God's purposes in those regions. This discernment comes through prayer, fasting, and listening to the Holy Spirit. Often, God will reveal the nature of the ruling spirit through patterns in the land: persistent idolatry, economic oppression, immorality, corruption, or bloodshed. In Acts 16, Paul identified the spirit of divination operating in a slave girl because the Holy Spirit made him aware of it, even though others may have seen it as harmless fortune-telling.

Without discernment, a believer may fight blindly and waste spiritual energy. When we identify the specific ruling spirit, we can address it with precision, using targeted intercession and scriptural decrees that strike at its roots. This stage is about diagnosis, knowing exactly what needs to be uprooted before planting God's kingdom.

2. Repentance and Cleansing of the Land

Once the ruling spirit is identified, the next move is to address any legal grounds that give it authority to remain. Demonic spirits are legalistic. They hold territory because of unrepented sin, covenantal agreements with false gods, or bloodshed that has not been spiritually addressed. This is why in 2 Chronicles 7:14, God says that His people must "humble themselves, pray, seek My face, and turn from their wicked ways" for the land to be healed.

Repentance can be personal, corporate, or even intercessory, as in Nehemiah 1 when Nehemiah confessed the sins of his fathers and the nation. Cleansing the land may involve renouncing past covenants, breaking soul ties with idolatrous traditions, or asking God to redeem sites where innocent blood has been shed. In the Old Testament, altars were often built to declare a new covenant with God over a location. Abraham, Jacob, and Joshua all did this.

This is a critical phase because without cleansing the land spiritually, believers may take physical control but still be resisted by entrenched powers. A cleansed land becomes spiritually available for God's presence and purposes to flourish without opposition from ancient claims.

3. Establishing God's Presence Through Worship and Declaration

When Joshua entered the Promised Land, one of his first recorded acts was to gather Israel for covenant renewal, reading the Law of God aloud (Joshua 8:30–35). This principle shows that after dealing with the enemy's claims, the territory must be filled with the presence of God. Worship, prayer, and public declaration of God's Word change the spiritual climate and invite divine authority to settle over the land.

In Acts 16, Paul and Silas sang hymns in prison, and God's power shook the place. Worship is not just music. It is a declaration of allegiance that dethrones demonic powers and enthrones God (Psalm 22:3). When believers worship openly over a territory, they shift the atmosphere, making it hostile to darkness.

Declarations are equally vital. Job 22:28 says, "You will decree a thing, and it will be established for you." Speaking God's promises over the land, whether about blessing, fruitfulness, or protection, sets the spiritual boundaries of the territory. These verbal decrees are like spiritual survey markers that say, "This land belongs to the Lord."

4. Strategic Prophetic Action

Throughout Scripture, God often instructed His people to carry out prophetic actions to signify spiritual realities. Moses stretched out his staff over the Red Sea (Exodus 14:16), Elisha threw salt into a spring to heal it (2 Kings 2:21), and Jesus anointed a blind man's eyes with mud (John 9:6). These were not empty rituals. They were physical expressions of spiritual authority that activated heaven's intervention.

When confronting territorial spirits, prophetic acts may involve walking the land in prayer, pouring oil as a sign of consecration, or planting Scripture-filled stakes in the ground as declarations of God's ownership. Joshua 1:3 states that every place the sole of your foot treads has been given to you; walking the land is not just symbolic, it's an act of claiming legal spiritual rights.

The key here is obedience. Prophetic acts must be Spirit-led, not superstitious mimicry. When done under God's direction, they serve as visible reminders to both the natural and spiritual realms that the land is no longer under the control of darkness, but is now claimed for the kingdom of God.

5. Sustained Spiritual Governance
Possessing land spiritually is not a one-time event, it requires ongoing governance. In Judges 2, Israel's failure to maintain spiritual vigilance allowed old enemies to reassert control over the land. Sustained governance means establishing a constant spiritual presence: ongoing prayer, teaching, and community discipleship that reinforces God's rule over the territory.

This governance often involves placing God-fearing leaders in positions of influence, creating systems of justice, and ensuring that economic, educational, and cultural life in the territory align with biblical principles. The church should function as the "ecclesia," the governing assembly that sets the moral and spiritual tone of the region (Matthew 16:19).

Without sustained governance, territorial spirits can slowly return, reestablish their influence, and undo years of spiritual work. The victory is not fully secured until the land is saturated with kingdom culture, and the next generation is trained to guard the inheritance.

The End-Time Context: The Nations as the Lord's Inheritance

The ultimate goal is stated in Revelation 11:15: "The kingdom of the world has become the kingdom of our Lord and of his Christ, and he shall reign forever and ever." Believers are not just holding ground until heaven. We are actively expanding the territory of God's reign on earth. Every plot of land, every region reclaimed from demonic influence, is a foretaste of that final transfer of ownership.

1. Joshua and the Fall of Jericho (Joshua 6)

Jericho was the gateway city to the Promised Land; fortified, impenetrable, and spiritually guarded by Canaanite deities tied to that territory. In natural terms, Israel had no siege engines or military advantage. Yet God gave Joshua an unconventional spiritual strategy: march around the city once daily for six days, then seven times on the seventh day, with priests blowing trumpets and the people shouting.

This was not merely a military maneuver. It was an

act of spiritual warfare. The seven days represented divine completeness, and the blowing of the shofar was a declaration of God's kingship over the land. The walls fell, not from human strength, but because the spiritual authority over Jericho was broken.

Once Jericho's spiritual stronghold was dismantled, the physical city was conquered. This teaches that to possess land in the natural, we must first dethrone the spiritual rulers that occupy it.

2. David and the Capture of Jerusalem (2 Samuel 5:6–9)

Jerusalem was under the control of the Jebusites, who taunted David, claiming even the "blind and the lame" could keep him out. This mocking wasn't just arrogance. It reflected the city's long-standing spiritual resistance. For centuries, Israel had failed to take full control of Jerusalem despite God's promise.

David sought the Lord and received the strategy to enter through the water shaft, bypassing the fortified walls. This was not only military brilliance, it also symbolized the Spirit's wisdom giving God's people access where others saw impossibility.

Jerusalem became the political and spiritual capital of Israel because a leader with covenant faith confronted the territorial resistance and claimed what God had already decreed. Possessing land begins with believing God's promise more than the enemy's taunts.

3. William Carey and the Gospel in India

In the late 1700s, India was spiritually dominated by deeply entrenched religious systems, idol worship, and oppressive practices like sati (widow burning). William Carey, a missionary from England, faced immense resistance, not only from locals, but also from colonial authorities who feared upsetting the power structures.

Through decades of persistent prayer, Bible translation into multiple Indian languages, and social reform, Carey dismantled spiritual strongholds that had dominated the land for centuries. His work eventually led to the abolition of sati and laid the foundation for India's Christian educational institutions.

Carey's story proves that land possession is not only about property deeds. It's about shifting the spiritual atmosphere so God's righteousness can flourish in a territory.

4. Charles Mully and the Transformation of Kenyan Land

Charles Mully, once a homeless boy in Kenya, became a millionaire businessman. In the 1980s, God called him to sell his businesses and dedicate his life to rescuing abandoned children. He purchased large tracts of land in Kenya, but the land was dry, barren, and hostile to agriculture. Through faith, strategic irrigation, and prayer walks over the property, Mully transformed the land into a lush, self-sustaining community. This not only fed thousands of children but demonstrated to local authorities and skeptics that God could reverse the curse over a territory.

In this case, land possession was accompanied by environmental redemption; a picture of how believers can literally bring "Eden" back into wasted places when they displace territorial resistance.

5. David Oyedepo and Faith Tabernacle in Nigeria

In the 1990s, Bishop David Oyedepo announced that God had instructed him to build the largest church auditorium in the world on land that was considered bush territory outside Lagos. Critics mocked the idea, and spiritually, the land was associated with poverty and disuse.

Through prophetic declarations, aggressive evangelism, and financial faith, Oyedepo and his congregation acquired and developed over 10,000 acres, building Faith Tabernacle and Covenant University. Today, the site is a thriving hub for education, worship, and commerce, transforming not just the land but the surrounding economy.

His testimony reveals that when believers obey God's

voice and confront both physical and spiritual resistance, they can turn neglected land into centers of kingdom influence.

Chapter 11

ଔ

The Superior Construct of the Human
Unveiling the Divine Design at the Quantum Level

1. The Human as Heaven's Masterpiece

From the first breath God breathed into Adam's nostrils (Genesis 2:7), humanity became the most advanced creation in the material and spiritual realms. No mountain, ocean, star, or galaxy has the capacity for thought, choice, or creativity, but man does. We were made in the **image (Hebrew: *tselem*, the exact form)** and **likeness (Hebrew: *demuth*, functional similarity)** of God. This means that our very nature is patterned after the Creator's own essence, making us the only physical beings capable of consciously engaging both material and spiritual laws.

David marveled at this in **Psalm 8:4–6,** declaring, *"What is man that You are mindful of him, and the son of man that You visit him? For You have made him a little low-*

er than Elohim, and crowned him with glory and honor. You have given him dominion over the works of Your hands." Man's design was not accidental. It was intentional, superior, and strategic. We are wired for **rulership**, engineered for **innovation**, and imbued with the **capacity to harness creation's raw power**.

2. Life at the Subatomic Level - The Divine Engineering

Modern science has discovered that the visible world is built from **subatomic particles:** protons, neutrons, electrons, and the more exotic quarks and leptons. At the smallest scale, reality is not solid, but a vast, dynamic field of **energy and probability**. Scripture hinted at this reality thousands of years ago: **Hebrews 11:3** says, *"The worlds were framed by the word of God, so that what is seen was not made out of things which are visible."*

This means the foundation of the material world is invisible energy obeying laws spoken by God. Quantum physics confirms that particles exist as possibilities until they are observed or interacted with, then they take form. This is why your words, thoughts, and faith matter: they influence matter at its most fundamental level. **Proverbs 18:21** wasn't poetic exaggeration when it said, *"Death and life are in the power of the tongue."* Your voice can literally collapse possibilities into reality.

3. The Quantum Nature of Man - Designed for Dominion

Your body is not just flesh and bone; it is a living **bio-electromagnetic system** powered by trillions of atoms, each vibrating with life. The average human body contains approximately **7 octillion atoms**. That's a seven followed by twenty-seven zeroes; each a miniature universe of energy. Every heartbeat, thought, and word sends ripples through this ocean of particles, interacting with the physical world.

Believers have an advantage because they understand that their **spirit** energizes their body, and their **faith** directs that energy. **Romans 8:11** says, *"The Spirit of Him who raised Jesus from the dead dwells in you, He… will also give life to your mortal bodies through His Spirit who dwells in you."* This life-giving force is not just theological, it's physical. The same Spirit that called galaxies into being resides in your cells, making your design infinitely superior to anything else in creation.

4. Harnessing Quantum Principles - Faith as a Material Force

Quantum physics tells us that particles respond to **intention and observation**; the famous "double-slit experiment" showed that matter behaves differently when observed. Scripture aligns perfectly: **Mark 11:23–24** teaches that if you believe and do not doubt, you will have what you say. Faith is the **spiritual equivalent of quantum collapse**. It focuses possibilities into manifested realities.

When Jesus calmed the storm (Mark 4:39), multiplied bread (Matthew 14:19-21), or walked on water (Matthew 14:25-29), He wasn't breaking natural laws, He was operating from a **higher set of laws.** He understood that the subatomic building blocks of creation respond to divine authority. Because *"as He is, so are we in this world"* (1 John 4:17), you and I are called to operate in the same dimension.

5. Practical Applications - How to Rule the Material World

Theology and physics converge in practical action. You can begin harnessing your God-given construct through:

> **1. Focused Thought** – The mind is a field generator; sustained, focused thought reshapes neural pathways and aligns physical outcomes. Philippians 4:8 teaches us to think on what is pure, lovely, and of good report, not just for moral health but to align reality with divine order.
>
> **2. Faith-Decrees** – Speak with the understanding that your words are vibrational

commands to matter. Begin declaring ownership, health, and provision with precision. **Job 22:28** says, *"You will also decree a thing, and it will be established for you."*

3. Spiritual Alignment – Sin scrambles your frequency, however holiness aligns you with the Creator's resonance. When you walk in obedience, you are "tuned" to Heaven's frequency and the material world responds favorably.

4. Strategic Action – Dominion is not only spoken, it is acted upon. Joshua still had to march around Jericho. Innovation, investment, and building are expressions of dominion.

6. The Unstoppable Believer - Quantum Dominion in Real Life

History is filled with believers who tapped into this reality. George Washington Carver, a man of deep Christian faith, prayed over peanuts and discovered over **300 uses** for them, transforming agriculture. Johann Kepler, a devout Christian astronomer, described his scientific work as "thinking God's thoughts after Him." These individuals understood that **humanity's superior construct** was not for survival but for stewardship and rulership of the earth.

When you understand your **divine quantum design,** fear of lack disappears. You stop begging God for what He's already placed within you, and you start **creating with Him.** The subatomic world is not random. It's wired to obey the voice of the sons of God. Creation itself is "groaning" for you to rise (Romans 8:19), because when you take your rightful place, the earth is blessed, healed, and restored.

※

11 Quantum Principles for Ruling the Material World
1. Wave-Particle Duality - Living in Two Realms

In quantum mechanics, light and matter have a dual nature. Sometimes they behave like solid particles: tangible, measurable objects. At other times, they act as waves, spreading energy invisibly through space. This strange duality reveals that the boundaries between the physical and non-physical are not as rigid as we once thought. For believers, this is a vivid scientific picture of our true nature. We live in physical bodies, but we are also spirit-beings connected to the invisible realm.

Jesus embodied this principle perfectly. In one moment, He was physically eating fish with His disciples (Luke 24:42–43), and in another, He was walking on water

(Matthew 14:25). He could pass through locked doors after His resurrection (John 20:19), yet still bear the scars in His hands and side. His life shows that a believer can operate in both dimensions, the material and the spiritual, without contradiction.

Practical Application: Wave-particle duality means that you are not limited to the visible conditions of your environment. You can function in your job, family, or community while simultaneously pulling solutions from Heaven's invisible storehouse. You can face a financial "particle" reality like lack and release a "wave" of faith that shifts the outcome. The key is to refuse to see yourself as only a natural being; you are a spirit ruling in a body.

2. Observer Effect - Faith Shapes Reality

The observer effect states that the very act of observation changes the outcome of a quantum event. When you look at a particle, it behaves differently than when you do not. In other words, expectation changes manifestation. This aligns perfectly with the biblical principle of faith.

Jesus told His disciples in Mark 11:24, "Whatever you ask for in prayer, believe that you have received it, and it will be yours." Faith is not passive belief, it is an active focus on a desired outcome until it manifests. Hebrews 11:1 defines faith as "the substance of things hoped for, the evidence of things not seen." When your spirit "observes" through faith, you influence the outcome of what will happen in the physical world.

Practical Application: If the world responds to observation at a subatomic level, then your spiritual attention and declarations matter. The believer who focuses on God's promises in the middle of crisis changes the "energy field" of their circumstances. You cannot afford random thoughts or idle words, every expectation is shaping tomorrow. Observation in the Spirit is intentional faith.

3. Quantum Entanglement - Divine Connectivity

Quantum entanglement describes a phenomenon where two particles, once connected, remain linked so that a change in one instantly affects the other no matter the distance between them. This is an astonishing picture of the spiritual unity believers share in Christ.

Paul writes in 1 Corinthians 12:26, "If one part suffers, every part suffers with it; if one part is honored, every part rejoices with it." This spiritual "entanglement" explains why prayer can have an immediate effect across continents and why the body of Christ functions as a living organism. Jesus also described this when He said, "I am the vine; you are the branches." (John 15:5)

Practical Application: Your prayers and prophetic

declarations can shift realities in another person's life because in the Spirit, you are connected. This also means that the unity of believers amplifies power. When the Church prays in agreement, they release changes in the "quantum fabric" of the earth. You are not an isolated Christian; you are a quantum-connected ambassador of Heaven.

4. Superposition - Multiple Possibilities Awaiting Faith

In quantum physics, superposition describes how a particle can exist in multiple potential states at once until it is measured. This means the future is full of possibilities, and which one manifests depends on how and when it is "observed" or acted upon.

Biblically, God sets before humanity multiple outcomes. In Deuteronomy 30:19, He declares, *"I have set before you life and death, blessings and curses. Now choose life."* Your choice, aligned with faith and obedience, "collapses" the possibilities into one reality. Superposition is the scientific mirror of divine free will and the role of faith in shaping destiny.

Practical Application: There are infinite scenarios for your life, but the one that manifests will be the one you agree with through your faith and actions. The promises of God are available to you like unobserved quantum states, but they must be "measured" through confession, obedience, and action. You are never trapped. There is always another reality waiting to be activated.

5. Quantum Tunneling - Passing Through Barriers
Quantum tunneling is the ability of a particle to pass through an obstacle that should be impenetrable according to classical physics. It's as if the laws of limitation bend for certain conditions.

Isaiah 43:16 speaks of God making "a way through the sea, a path through the mighty waters." This is quantum tunneling in action on a macro scale. The Red Sea parting, walls of Jericho collapsing, and Peter walking out of prison after chains fell off are divine demonstrations of matter yielding to higher authority.

Practical Application: Believers face "walls" in finances, health, and relationships that appear unbreakable. But faith allows you to tunnel through them, not by ignoring natural laws, but by engaging a higher spiritual law. Every seemingly impossible situation is simply matter waiting to yield to the voice of the Creator in you.

6. Energy-Matter Equivalence ($E=mc^2$) - Transformation, Not Destruction
Einstein's famous formula shows that matter and energy are interchangeable forms of the same reality. This means nothing is truly destroyed, it is transformed.

In 1 Corinthians 15:53, Paul describes resurrection

as the perishable putting on the imperishable. The believer's body is not erased, but transformed into a glorified form. The same power that raised Jesus from the dead (Romans 8:11) is available to transform circumstances, resources, and even your own life trajectory.

Practical Application: This principle means no loss is final. What you think is "gone" may simply be in another form, waiting to be called back into usefulness. A failed business can become wisdom capital. A broken relationship can become a ministry testimony. Energy and matter are two sides of the same coin. God can flip them at will.

7. Quantum Coherence - The Power of Alignment

Coherence happens when particles are in harmony (aligned in phase) causing their effects to amplify dramatically.

In Acts 2:1–4, the early Church was "all together in one place," and the Spirit came in explosive power. This is spiritual coherence. The alignment of hearts, minds, and words releases exponential results in prayer, business, and relationships.

Practical Application: Coherence explains why discord weakens churches, families, and even teams at work. When you align your thoughts, words, and actions with God's will, you enter spiritual coherence, and results come faster and stronger. Alignment is not just agreement. It's unified direction.

8. Quantum Fluctuations - Creation from the Invisible

In physics, quantum fluctuations describe how energy in "empty" space can create matter spontaneously.

Romans 4:17 tells us God *"calls into being things that were not."* In Genesis 1, the universe was formless and void, but God's word brought matter from what seemed like nothing. There is no true emptiness in creation, only potential waiting for a command.

Practical Application: When your life seems empty, it is actually rich with invisible potential. Your declarations, ideas, and actions are the "energy inputs" that give rise to visible results. You are never starting from zero. You are starting from unseen abundance.

9. Planck Scale Limits - Beyond Time and Space

The Planck scale defines the smallest possible length and time, beyond which our usual concepts of physics break down. At that point, the universe is no longer bound by time and space as we understand them.

2 Peter 3:8 reminds us that "with the Lord a day is like a thousand years, and a thousand years are like a day." God is not constrained by time or distance. He operates both inside and outside creation's limits.

Practical Application: Your prayers are not delayed

because of distance or time zones. You can receive "instant answers" because God operates beyond the Planck scale. Understanding this frees you from the frustration of earthly clocks, you live in eternal timing.

10. Quantum Resonance - The Frequency of Heaven

Resonance occurs when one frequency amplifies another, producing a powerful effect.

Psalm 22:3 says God is enthroned on the praises of His people. Worship is resonance; our spirit aligning with Heaven's frequency. When this happens, divine power is amplified into our environment, shifting atmospheres and circumstances.

Practical Application: You can tune your life to resonate with God through worship, gratitude, and speaking His Word. This is not emotional hype; it's frequency alignment. The more you resonate with Heaven, the more Heaven manifests in your physical reality.

11. Quantum Leap - Instant Dimensional Shift

In quantum physics, a quantum leap is the sudden transition of a particle from one discrete energy state to another without traveling the intermediate path. It is not gradual. It is immediate. The "rules" of the previous level no longer apply once the leap is made. This defies our usual concepts of linear progress, where we expect slow, step-by-step advancement.

Biblically, we see quantum leaps in moments when God bypasses natural processes. Joseph went from prisoner to prime minister in a single day (Genesis 41:39–41). David went from shepherd boy to national hero after one battle with Goliath (1 Samuel 17:50–51). The woman with the issue of blood leaped from 12 years of sickness into instantaneous healing the moment she touched Jesus' garment (Mark 5:29). In each case, the leap was triggered by a decisive act of either faith, obedience, or divine appointment.

Why This Matters for Believers

The quantum leap principle teaches believers that not all growth or success must be gradual. The Kingdom of God allows for accelerated transitions when the right spiritual "energy" (faith, obedience, alignment with God's timing) is applied. Just as in physics, the leap happens when enough energy is absorbed. Spiritually, this energy is the power of the Holy Spirit igniting faith.

Practical Application

Faith as the Energy Input – Just as an electron absorbs energy before leaping, you absorb spiritual power through prayer, fasting, and the Word. When your inner capacity reaches critical mass, the leap happens.

Obedience as the Trigger – The leap is not random. It happens in response to obedience to divine instruction. Peter experienced a quantum leap in his fishing business when he obeyed Jesus' command to cast the net again (Luke 5:4–6).

Bypassing Natural Timelines – Expect God to bypass the "necessary steps" others say you must take. A quantum leap can catapult you over years of waiting into a position of influence, ownership, or ministry impact in a moment.

Quantum Principles Conclusion: Resonating Reality - How Thoughts and Words Shift Matter

At the subatomic level, all matter is made of energy, and energy responds to frequency. Thoughts generate measurable energy patterns. Words, spoken with intent, are vibrational releases that ripple through the unseen realm and strike the quantum fabric of creation. In the same way a tuning fork can cause glass to shatter by matching its resonant frequency, your mind and mouth can release waves that cause the matter in your environment to rearrange itself to match the pattern you declare.

Scripture has been saying this long before quantum physics could name it. Proverbs 18:21 declares, "Death and life are in the power of the tongue, and those who love it will eat its fruits." Your words are not harmless syllables, they are containers of spiritual energy. They move through the "field" of your reality, collapsing possibilities into chosen outcomes. Jesus demonstrated this mastery when He spoke to storms (Mark 4:39), cursed fig trees (Mark 11:14), and even called a dead man out of the grave (John 11:43–44). Each word was a frequency release that matter obeyed without negotiation.

The believer's thoughts are the seedbed for these words. What you meditate on determines the frequency of your inner atmosphere. Philippians 4:8 tells us to think on what is true, noble, right, pure, lovely, and admirable. This is not mere moral advice, it is a divine engineering manual for setting your inner frequency to Heaven's wavelength. A mind aligned with God's truth produces words that resonate with Heaven's resonance, and Heaven's resonance always overpowers the static of fear, lack, and death.

When you speak in faith, you are not wishing for change, you are engaging the architecture of reality. Just as light waves can bend matter at the microscopic level, the wave of a God-breathed declaration can bend circumstances at the macroscopic level. Your "Let there be..." echoes the Creator's first command in Genesis 1:3, and creation responds because you are speaking from His delegated authority. The earth's atoms still remember the sound of His voice, and when you speak in alignment with Him, they hear that sound again.

So, do not speak carelessly. Every thought is a pre-word, and every word is a launched particle of power. You are a living transmitter, a resonator of the Kingdom, and the material world is tuned to respond to you when you are tuned to God. The state of your life right now is the crystallization of past words and dominant thoughts. Change the frequency, and you change the form. As a believer, this is not optional. It is your mandate. Speak light into darkness, order into chaos, abundance into lack, and watch as the quantum particles of the material world shift, align, and serve your destiny - even in the marketplace.

☙

Believers as Kingdom Pioneers in the Marketplace
From the beginning, God established humanity as His co-regents on earth. In Genesis 1:28, the Creator's first recorded words to mankind were a mandate for dominion: *"Be fruitful and multiply, fill the earth and subdue it; have dominion over... every living thing."* This was not a call to passive existence; it was a royal commission to lead, innovate, and expand. Dominion requires initiative, vision,

and mastery of resources. Believers are not merely called to survive in the world, they are called to shape it. Every technological advancement, business empire, and cultural shift is either stewarded for the glory of God or hijacked by darkness. When believers refuse to lead in innovation and enterprise, they forfeit the stewardship of cultural influence to those without the fear of God.

The Kingdom of God is not a reactionary system. It is an initiatory one. Jesus described it as yeast that works through the whole dough (Matthew 13:33). Yeast doesn't sit idly, it permeates, transforms, and expands its environment until everything is affected by its presence. If believers are truly the *"light of the world"* (Matthew 5:14), then they should be the first to illuminate new pathways in science, technology, art, economics, and governance. Light doesn't wait for darkness to move, it shines first. The biblical standard is that God's people set the pace of human advancement, not follow the trends dictated by the ungodly.

Entrepreneurship and innovation are simply modern expressions of biblical stewardship. Jesus' parable of the talents (Matthew 25:14–30) reveals God's expectation for increase. The master commended the servants who multiplied what was entrusted to them and condemned the one who played it safe. The Kingdom honors multiplication, not stagnation. Believers who create new businesses, invent solutions, and generate wealth are fulfilling a divine pattern; transforming resources into greater impact. In a world plagued by poverty, corruption, and inequity, Spirit-filled innovators are desperately needed to model ethical success and Kingdom generosity.

Financial dominance in the hands of righteous people is a strategic weapon for advancing God's purposes. Ecclesiastes 9:16 laments that *"the poor man's wisdom is despised, and his words are not heard."* This is not because wisdom loses its value, but because influence follows resources. The wealth of the wicked is laid up for the righteous (Proverbs 13:22), but it must be claimed through vision, diligence, and skill, not wishful thinking. Billionaire believers are not a luxury; they are a necessity for funding missions, shaping industries, influencing laws, and discipling nations. Without economic leadership, the Church remains dependent on systems it should be governing.

Believers have the advantage of divine insight. James 1:5 promises wisdom to those who ask, and this wisdom is not limited to sermons and church administration. It also applies to patents, product development, disruptive technologies, and creative strategies that shift industries. The Holy Spirit is the Spirit of truth (John 16:13) and creativity, the same Spirit who empowered Bezalel to craft the intricate tabernacle design (Exodus 31:1–5). Every revolutionary idea in history, from the printing press to modern medicine, was birthed in the mind of someone made in God's image. How much more should Spirit-filled believers, in direct communion with the Creator, lead in pioneering breakthroughs?

Cultural influence flows from thought leadership. Proverbs 29:18 says, *"Where there is no vision, the people perish."* Visionaries dictate the future because they see what others cannot yet imagine. For too long, the Church has limited its brightest minds to pulpits and pews, neglecting boardrooms, laboratories, media studios, and legislative halls. Thought leaders determine the values, narratives, and possibilities a society embraces. If believers are absent from these arenas, the ideologies that govern nations will inevitably drift from righteousness. The call is clear: believers must be the ones producing the ideas, not just responding to them.

Innovation is not a secular concept, it is a Kingdom trait. God is the ultimate Creator, and as His offspring (Acts 17:28), we are wired to create. Every invention, breakthrough, or pioneering venture is an act of subduing the earth and revealing God's wisdom to principalities and powers (Ephesians 3:10). This is why Daniel, even as an exile in Babylon, outperformed every pagan advisor ten times over (Daniel 1:20). The same Spirit that distinguished

Daniel resides in believers today. The world should look to the Church for the next agricultural revolution, the next medical breakthrough, the next technological leap because God's people carry Heaven's blueprint for earthly transformation.

Finally, being at the forefront of innovation, enterprise, and influence is not about personal glory. It is about Kingdom manifestation. Jesus taught us to pray, *"Your Kingdom come, Your will be done on earth as it is in Heaven"* (Matthew 6:10). In Heaven, there is no poverty, no oppression, no stunted potential. For that reality to be mirrored on earth, believers must occupy the high places of decision-making and resource distribution. Innovation and wealth in righteous hands translate into schools built, clean water systems installed, unjust laws overturned, and the gospel advanced without financial restraint. Believers are not called to compete for scraps in the world's systems. They are called to build the systems.

Dominion Through Mastery of the Unseen Realm

The true foundation of believer dominion is not mere intellect, talent, or hard work, it is mastery over the unseen realm. Hebrews 11:3 declares, *"By faith we understand that the universe was created by the word of God, so that what is seen was not made out of things that are visible."* Everything tangible in the material world has its origin in the invisible. Matter itself is a manifestation of unseen energy, shaped by the Word of God. This means that the believer who understands and governs the spiritual laws of the invisible realm wields a higher authority than any earthly system, because the unseen governs the seen.

When Joshua commanded the sun to stand still (Joshua 10:12-14), he was not just making a poetic request, he was exercising jurisdiction over the cosmic order by the authority of God. Time, light, planetary motion, laws that scientists deem unbreakable, bent in obedience to a man who was aligned with Heaven's purposes. The Scripture emphasizes that *"there has been no day like it before or since, when the LORD heeded the voice of a man."* This is the level of dominion believers are called to walk in: speaking Heaven's decrees into the earth with such precision that the natural order responds. If the Old Covenant warrior Joshua could operate at this dimension, how much more the New Covenant sons of God, indwelt by the Creator Himself?

Jesus demonstrated this mastery repeatedly. He calmed a storm with a word (Mark 4:39), turned water into wine (John 2:1-11), multiplied loaves and fish (Matthew 14:13-21), and commanded a fig tree to wither (Mark 11:14, 20-21). Each act was a visible display of authority over the laws of nature, rooted in His union with the Father and His understanding of spiritual laws. He was showing us not only who He is, but who we are meant to be: partners in dominion, governing the visible world by governing the invisible forces behind it.

This is why believers are uniquely positioned to be the **chief innovators, entrepreneurs, thought leaders, billionaires, and pioneers.** True innovation does not begin in a laboratory. It begins in the realm of ideas, visions, and divine downloads from the Spirit of God. The quantum-level reality of the universe affirms what Scripture has always declared: the invisible blueprint shapes the visible outcome. Spirit-led believers, filled with the Creator's mind, can access strategies, inventions, and solutions before they are ever conceived by the world's greatest think tanks.

Our words, aligned with God's will, have creative force. Proverbs 18:21 teaches that *"death and life are in the power of the tongue."* Job 22:28 declares, *"You will also decree a thing, and it will be established for you; and light will shine on your ways."* These are not symbolic statements, they are operational principles for exercising dominion. Speaking to matter, commanding outcomes, and aligning the material world with Kingdom purposes is the believer's birthright. Whether it is commanding a disease to leave, calling forth resources, redirecting a storm, or unlocking a breakthrough in technology, we act as Heaven's representatives in the earth.

This mastery over the unseen realm is not a privilege for an elite few, it is the inheritance of every son and daughter of God. Romans 8:19 says, *"For the creation waits with eager longing for the revealing of the sons of God."* The earth itself is waiting for people who understand how to operate in the laws of the invisible world, so they can bring the visible world into alignment with Heaven. The systems, wealth, and lands of the earth are not just waiting to be claimed. They are waiting to be governed by those who walk in spiritual authority. And when the righteous rise into this role, they do not just take territory, they transform it for the glory of God.

Chapter 12

Strategies for Supernaturally Manipulating the Laws of the Material World

The material world is not a self-contained, untouchable realm. It is governed by higher, invisible laws that the believer can access and employ. As children of God, we have the authority to influence, reorder, and command the visible realm to align with Heaven's purposes. This is not mysticism, it is Kingdom technology, rooted in biblical principles and the power of the Holy Spirit. The following strategies are both spiritual and practical disciplines that give us mastery over the systems of the earth.

1. Fasting - Recalibrating the Spirit for Supernatural Authority

Fasting is one of the most underestimated spiritual weapons for manipulating the laws of the material world. Jesus

Himself connected fasting to supernatural power when He told His disciples in Matthew 17:21, *"This kind does not go out except by prayer and fasting."* Fasting empties the body of distractions and heightens spiritual perception, making it easier to hear divine instructions that bypass natural limitations.

When you fast, your spirit comes into dominance over the demands of the flesh. This sharpens your ability to sense the flow of divine strategy; when to speak, when to act, and when to wait. Many breakthroughs in history came during or after a period of fasting: Moses receiving the Law, Daniel receiving visions, and Jesus launching His ministry after forty days in the wilderness. Fasting puts you in a frequency of Heaven that allows you to see the material world from the Creator's perspective.

On a practical level, fasting shifts focus from human effort to divine empowerment. It disengages you from the noise of the world and recalibrates your inner compass. In this posture, you are no longer reacting to the material world, you are proactively shaping it through Spirit-led decisions and decrees.

2. Meditation, Decrees, and Commanded Prayers

Meditation on the Word of God is not passive. It is an active engagement of the mind and spirit with divine truth until it becomes your default operating system. Joshua 1:8 tells us that meditation produces prosperity and success because it rewrites your inner blueprint, aligning your thoughts with Heaven's design.

Decrees and declarations take this further. Job 22:28 says, *"You will also declare a thing, and it will be established for you; so light will shine on your ways."* When you decree, you are not making a request, you are issuing a legal order in the spirit that the material world must obey. This is the same pattern Jesus followed when He said, *"Peace, be still!"* to the storm (Mark 4:39).

Commands are the highest form of prayer when dealing with creation or demonic resistance. You are not asking, you are enforcing. Whether it is calling forth resources, commanding sickness to leave, or releasing favor into a business transaction, your words are containers of power that shape reality. In this way, meditation fills you with truth, and decrees release that truth into the material world as tangible outcomes.

3. Prophetic Planning - Aligning Vision with Divine Timing

Prophetic planning is the art of merging divine revelation with strategic execution. Proverbs 16:3 says, "Commit your work to the LORD, and your plans will be established." This does not mean we abandon planning, it means our plans must be Spirit-breathed.

Every move of God on earth involved detailed preparation: Noah's ark was built to exact specifications; Joseph stored grain for seven years based on a prophetic dream; David organized the temple's construction years before Solomon built it. Prophetic planning requires listening for divine blueprints and timing, so that when you act, you act in sync with Heaven's calendar.

This strategy manipulates the material world because it positions you ahead of natural events. You don't just react to economic shifts, you prepare for them before they occur. You don't just respond to opportunity, you create it by aligning your plans with God's foreknowledge. The result is that resources, people, and circumstances converge at the right time for maximum impact.

4. Development of Skills for Strategic Work

While supernatural authority is spiritual, the execution often requires natural skill. Exodus 31:3–5 tells us that Bezalel was "filled with the Spirit of God, in wisdom, in understanding, in knowledge, and in all manner of workmanship" to build the Tabernacle. The Spirit anointed his craftsmanship to create what had never existed before.

Skills, whether in business, technology, negotiation,

or creative arts, become supernatural tools when surrendered to God. A believer who pairs spiritual authority with professional excellence becomes unstoppable. Skills give credibility in the marketplace and expand your influence in spheres that might otherwise resist spiritual authority.

Investing in personal development is not a lack of faith, it is an act of stewardship. Your skills are the handles God uses to turn Kingdom revelation into material reality. When a prophetic word meets a skilled hand, innovation happens, industries shift, and entire economies can be influenced for the Kingdom.

5. Strategic Alliances - Building Networks that Multiply Impact

No one possesses the world alone. Even Jesus chose twelve and moved within relational networks that multiplied His influence. Ecclesiastes 4:9–12 declares, "Two are better than one… a cord of three strands is not quickly broken." Strategic alliances allow you to access resources, skills, and territories you could never reach alone.

Forging these alliances requires discernment. Align yourself with people who share Kingdom values but also carry complementary strengths. This could mean partnering with business leaders, innovators, intercessors, or community influencers who are positioned in the very systems you seek to influence.

Strategic alliances manipulate the material world by creating power blocs that shift cultural, political, or economic climates. In unity, believers can leverage collective wisdom, financial capacity, and spiritual authority to possess land, dominate industries, and establish righteous governance in strategic territories.

6. Worship as a Warfare Technology
One often-overlooked strategy is worship. Worship changes atmospheres faster than any natural method because it enthrones God in a place (Psalm 22:3). When God is enthroned, every opposing force must bow. Jehoshaphat's army in 2 Chronicles 20 won a battle through worship before they ever raised a sword. Territorial enemies destroyed themselves while Judah sang praises.

Worship manages the laws of the material world by inviting the Creator to exercise direct dominion over the creation. It destabilizes demonic control and ushers in divine order, making it easier for you to step into possession of what God has assigned to you.

7. Prophetic Acts and Symbolic Actions
Throughout Scripture, God's people performed prophetic acts that shifted the material realm: Moses stretching his

rod over the Red Sea, Joshua marching around Jericho, Elisha throwing salt into bitter water. These actions were not mere rituals, they were faith-charged commands that reordered physical matter according to spiritual law.

Prophetic acts are powerful because they provide a point of contact between the invisible and visible realms. When performed in obedience to God's instruction, they can dislodge entrenched opposition and unlock supernatural access to land, resources, and influence.

The material world is not a self-contained, untouchable realm, it is governed by higher, invisible laws that the believer can access and employ. As children of God, we have the authority to influence, reorder, and command the visible realm to align with Heaven's purposes. This is not mysticism. It is Kingdom technology, rooted in biblical principles and the power of the Holy Spirit. The following strategies are both spiritual and practical disciplines that give us mastery over the systems of the earth.

Chapter 13
❧

Territorial Dominion and Generational Wealth Transfer

From the beginning, God designed the earth not merely to be inhabited but to be governed by His image-bearers. Dominion was not a suggestion; it was a mandate. In Genesis 1:28, God blessed humanity and commanded, *"Be fruitful and multiply, fill the earth and subdue it; have dominion…"* This means that the believer's destiny is tied to influence over land, culture, resources, and systems. The spiritual authority we carry is not confined to personal victories. It extends to the transformation of entire territories and the transfer of wealth from unrighteous stewardship into the hands of the righteous.

1. Understanding Territorial Dominion
Territorial dominion is more than geographical control; it

is the spiritual and practical mastery of a sphere of influence. A "territory" can be a nation, city, industry, or market sector. Proverbs 29:2 says, "When the righteous increase, the people rejoice." God's plan is for His people to rise to positions where they can set policies, shift culture, and implement Kingdom values that bless entire populations.

Daniel is a perfect example. Captured in Babylon, he operated with such divine excellence and supernatural wisdom that kings depended on him for national stability. His position gave him influence over the laws, economic structures, and religious freedoms of the land. This is not accidental, it's a pattern. God elevates those who steward their spiritual authority and practical skills to reshape nations.

2. The Spiritual Basis for Wealth Transfer

Wealth transfer is not a prosperity cliché, it is a scriptural certainty. Proverbs 13:22 tells us, "The wealth of the sinner is stored up for the righteous." This is not simply about money changing hands; it is about control of resources, institutions, and innovations being entrusted to those who will use them for the glory of God.

In Egypt, Joseph orchestrated one of the greatest wealth transfers in history. Through prophetic insight and administrative genius, he moved an empire's economy into Pharaoh's control, positioning himself as the chief steward of the world's grain supply. In our day, such transfer may manifest as business acquisitions, intellectual property rights, real estate control, and influence in global markets.

3. How Dominion and Wealth Intersect

Dominion without resources is limited; resources without dominion can be wasted. The two must work together. When believers take dominion over a territory, whether a literal region or a cultural sphere, they position themselves to steward its wealth. This wealth, in turn, becomes a tool for sustaining influence.

The early church understood this synergy. Acts 4:34–35 records that there were no needy among them because those who owned lands or houses sold them and laid the proceeds at the apostles' feet for Kingdom distribution. Dominion here was not abstract; it was tangible, economic, and transformative.

Strategies for Securing Territorial Influence and Dominance

To operate in territorial dominion, believers must move intentionally. The conquest of territory, whether spiritual, economic, social, or political, is never accidental. It is the product of intentional, Spirit-led strategy. In the Kingdom of God, dominance is not about oppression but stewardship; not about exploitation but righteous governance. Below are key strategies every believer must master to secure and sustain territorial influence.

1. Discerning the Spiritual Climate Before Engagement

Before Israel ever marched into Canaan, God sent spies to survey the land (Numbers 13). This reconnaissance was not merely for military logistics; it was a spiritual intelligence mission. Every territory has a spiritual climate, a unique blend of cultural values, prevailing mindsets, demonic gatekeepers, and potential Kingdom allies. You cannot dominate what you have not discerned.

Believers must pray, fast, and seek prophetic insight before making territorial moves. This could mean studying market trends before launching a business, analyzing the political climate before stepping into civic influence, or identifying the spiritual strongholds of a city before planting a church. Joshua was told to "be strong and very courageous" (Joshua 1:7), but that courage was fueled by a clear understanding of the land's challenges and opportunities.

When you discern the spiritual climate, you know what to confront, what to cultivate, and what to capitalize on. This is the difference between moving blindly and moving with prophetic precision.

2. Establishing an Unshakable Spiritual Presence

Every territorial power understands one thing: whoever controls the altar controls the land. In the Old Testament, altars were not only places of worship but territorial claims. Abraham built an altar in Shechem (Genesis 12:7) and effectively marked it as Kingdom territory. Elijah rebuilt the altar on Mount Carmel before calling down fire (1 Kings 18:30), re-establishing God's authority over Israel.

In modern contexts, our "altars" are not stone monuments but consistent, strategic spiritual engagements of prayer gatherings, worship events, prophetic declarations, and Kingdom-driven service initiatives. These activities shift atmospheres, drive out demonic occupiers, and release angelic assistance. When your presence in a territory is marked by constant spiritual activity, the enemy knows you are not a visitor, you are an occupier.

Sustained prayer walks, regular corporate worship in strategic locations, and prophetic decrees over a city's economy, culture, and leadership form an unshakable spiritual presence that keeps darkness displaced.

3. Embedding Kingdom Influence in Cultural Systems

It is not enough to hold spiritual gatherings while leaving the systems of culture untouched. If the education system is dominated by godless ideologies, if the arts and media glorify corruption, if business sectors are run on greed, the spiritual strongholds will remain intact.

Kingdom dominance requires placing Spirit-filled believers in positions of influence across the Seven Mountains of culture: religion, family, education, government, media, arts/entertainment, and business. This is exactly what Daniel did in Babylon. He didn't just pray in his room, he became the chief advisor to kings. Joseph didn't just interpret dreams, he became the Prime Minister of Egypt. Esther didn't just fast, she influenced royal decrees that saved her people.

When believers infiltrate these systems with Kingdom values, they begin to set the moral, ethical, and economic temperature of a territory. This is not infiltration for personal gain, but for the exaltation of God's will in the public square.

4. Fortifying the Economy of the Territory

A territory cannot be truly dominated if its economy is controlled by hostile forces. In Scripture, the wealth of a land determined its strength and influence. When Israel obeyed God, He blessed their fields, flocks, and trade (Deuteronomy 28:12). When they disobeyed, foreign powers drained their resources.

Believers must understand that economic control is

a form of spiritual control. This means pioneering businesses, controlling supply chains, investing strategically, and creating economic ecosystems that fund Kingdom work. This is what Joseph did when he stored grain during Egypt's years of plenty; when famine struck, not only did Egypt survive, but it became the world's breadbasket.

Securing territorial dominance means breaking dependency on godless economic structures. It means raising entrepreneurs, investors, and innovators who can supply the city with goods, services, and jobs ensuring the land flourishes under righteous stewardship.

5. Raising and Empowering Local Leadership

True dominance is not maintained by one charismatic figure but by a network of trained, empowered leaders who share the same vision and values. Moses learned this when Jethro advised him to appoint capable men over thousands, hundreds, fifties, and tens (Exodus 18:21).

Raising local leaders ensures the territory is not dependent on imported influence but thrives with indigenous strength. These leaders should be equipped not only in spiritual matters but in governance, economic management, and cultural engagement. When local leadership is Kingdom-aligned, the territory becomes resistant to external manipulation.

Empowering leaders is also a form of succession planning ensuring that even if one leader is removed, the vision continues without interruption.

6. Guarding the Gates - Spiritual and Physical

In biblical times, the gates of a city were both literal and symbolic. They were the points of entry for trade, governance, and ideas. The enemy often seeks to infiltrate through the "gates" of a territory: influential leaders, strategic industries, major media platforms, and even physical infrastructure.

Believers must guard these gates through intercession, policy influence, and active engagement. Nehemiah understood this when he stationed guards at Jerusalem's gates to protect it from attack (Nehemiah 7:3). In our time, guarding the gates may mean ensuring righteous oversight of key institutions, regulating what content enters a community, or protecting the minds of the next generation through Kingdom-based education.

If you do not control the gates, you will eventually lose control of the city - no matter how strong your spiritual presence is.

7. Building Strategic Alliances

No territory is conquered alone. Even David, a mighty warrior, needed the loyalty of his mighty men. Paul had ministry partners like Barnabas, Silas, and Priscilla and Aquila. Strategic alliances amplify resources, influence, and capacity for impact. These alliances can be with other Kingdom leaders, sympathetic civic leaders, or even non-believers whose values align with righteousness in specific initiatives. The key is discernment; aligning with those whose involvement will advance, not dilute, the Kingdom agenda.

Well-forged alliances can accelerate the transformation of a territory, protect your influence from attack, and open doors to realms of society you could never access alone.

❧

Prophetic Warfare: The Decree of Territorial Possession
In the name of the Lord Jesus Christ, we declare that the earth is the Lord's, and the fullness thereof; the world, and they that dwell therein (Psalm 24:1). Every square mile of land is under the Creator's title deed, and as His heirs, we stand as rightful possessors of what has been entrusted to the Kingdom. No demon, no principality, no human system has the eternal right to hold territory that God has destined for His glory.

We stand as sons and daughters of the Most High, authorized to subdue, replenish, and have dominion (Genesis 1:28). We lift our voices like Joshua before Jericho, decreeing that every wall of resistance must fall. We declare over our cities, nations, and regions that the altars of darkness are overthrown, the gates are reclaimed, and the thrones of unrighteousness are dismantled.

We bind the territorial prince that wars against our inheritance, and we loose the resources, wealth, influence, and open doors that belong to us by covenant right. We decree that our presence is not temporary but permanent, our influence is not fleeting but generational, and our reign is not contested but established.

By prophetic decree, we align the heavens and the earth over our assigned regions. We summon angelic hosts to guard our borders, secure our gates, and enforce Heaven's government on earth. We release the sound of Kingdom authority into the atmosphere until the systems of this world become the Kingdoms of our Lord and of His Christ, and He shall reign forever and ever (Revelation 11:15).

This is our land. This is our assignment. This is our covenant right. We will possess it, cultivate it, and rule it for the glory of our King. And every opposing spirit, structure, and system will bow, not to our name, but to the name that is above every name: Jesus Christ, the Lord of all territories.

Principles of Generational Wealth

Wealth transfer must not end with one generation. Proverbs 13:22 emphasizes leaving an inheritance for children's children. This requires more than cash. It includes intellectual capital, business systems, real estate portfolios, leadership succession plans, and moral values that safeguard the wealth.

Abraham understood this. His covenant blessings were secured for Isaac and Jacob, ensuring that each generation began wealthier and more strategically positioned than the last. In modern terms, this might mean establishing trusts, teaching financial literacy in your family, and positioning heirs to inherit influence, not just assets.

Overcoming Resistance

Dominion and wealth transfer are never uncontested. Spiritual forces, corrupt systems, and competing interests will resist. The Canaanites did not leave their land willingly; Israel had to fight for it under divine instruction. Likewise, believers must be prepared for strategic warfare, spiritual and natural, to occupy what God has promised.

This is why the authority we carry from Chapter 11's principles is essential. Fasting, prophetic decrees, skill development, and strategic alliances are not just survival tools, they are conquest tools.

Living as Custodians, Not Consumers

True Kingdom wealth is custodial, not consumptive. We are stewards, not hoarders. God's aim is not for His people to amass resources for selfish indulgence but to fund Kingdom projects, rescue the oppressed, advance the gospel, and transform nations.

Solomon's wealth built the Temple, a monument that drew global attention to the God of Israel. Modern Kingdom entrepreneurs must see their ventures as platforms for influence, evangelism, and social reformation.

The Call to Rule

We are not waiting for the world to hand us influence, we are mandated to take it. Through supernatural mastery of the laws of the invisible realm and strategic excellence in the visible realm, believers become the architects of history. This is the era for sons and daughters of God to rise as the **chief innovators, entrepreneurs, policy-makers, billionaires, and pioneers of the age.**

When Joshua commanded the sun to stand still (Joshua 10:12–13), it was more than a miracle, it was a declaration that the created order must serve the purposes of the righteous. That same dominion mandate rests on us. The earth is waiting, the resources are available, and the Spirit of God is empowering. All that remains is for us to act.

Prophetic Declaration: Rising to Possess the Earth

I decree that we are not servants to the systems of this world, we are sons and heirs of the Most High God. The same Spirit that raised Christ from the dead quickens our mortal bodies, enlightens our minds, and empowers our hands for conquest. We stand as ambassadors of Heaven, custodians of Kingdom wealth, and rulers over territories appointed by God.

I declare that no principality, no territorial spirit, no demonic gatekeeper can withhold from us what Heaven has decreed is ours. Every land, every industry, every sphere assigned to us comes under the dominion of Christ through our obedience and boldness. Like Joshua, we command creation to align with the will of God; like Joseph, we manage the resources of nations with supernatural insight; like Daniel, we influence kings and shape empires by the wisdom of God.

I prophesy that the wealth of the wicked is being released into the hands of the righteous, not for vanity, but for vision; not for self-exaltation, but for the exaltation of the King of kings. We will build schools, reform justice systems, fund missions, innovate technologies, and restore broken cities.

I speak over this generation: Rise, sons and daughters of God! Step into your inheritance. Rule in the midst of your enemies. Possess the gates of your enemies. Be the head and not the tail, above only and never beneath. You are masters over the unseen realm and influencers in the visible realm. You command both the material and the spiritual world to serve the purposes of Heaven.

And so, we declare in unity: **The earth is the Lord's and the fullness thereof, and we, His sons, will manifest His rule until the kingdoms of this world become the Kingdom of our Lord and of His Christ. And He shall reign forever and ever. Amen.**

Chapter 14
ଔ
Today Is Your Birthday: Ask a Big Gift

Kings Make Big Requests – Pray audacious prayers!
Scripture's most audacious invitation doesn't whisper; it thunders. It is God Himself, Maker of galaxies, Governor of nations, pressing a blank check into the hands of His Son and saying, "Ask."

> Hear the voice of the enthronement Psalm:
> "I will declare the decree: the LORD hath said unto me, **Thou art my Son; this day have I begotten thee. Ask of me, and I shall give thee the heathen for thine inheritance, and the uttermost parts of the earth for thy possession. Thou shalt break them with a rod of iron; thou shalt dash them in pieces like a potter's vessel. Be wise now therefore, O ye kings: be instruct-

ed, ye judges of the earth." (Psalm 2:7–10, KJV)

This is coronation language. *"This day"* is the day of enthronement, the royal **birthday** of the King. On that day the Father does not say, *"Be careful, ask small."* He says, ***"Ask of Me… the ends of the earth."*** Size is the point. Scope is the point. Nations, not neighborhoods; the uttermost parts, not the next block. The Father's offer is as wide as the world and as long as history.

Now the shock: in Christ, **this decree is ours**. The New Testament reads Psalm 2 through the lens of Jesus' resurrection and exaltation (Acts 13:33; Hebrews 1:5). The Son has asked and received. But He has also made us **co-heirs** (Romans 8:17), seated us **with Him** (Ephesians 2:6), and handed us the Great Commission as the practical outworking of Psalm 2's scope (Matthew 28:18–20). If we are in the Son, then **His birthday** decree is our prayer vocabulary. Today, and every day in Christ, is our enthronement day. **Ask.**

A New Vocabulary for Royal Prayer
If sons and daughters pray like kings and queens, our language must expand. We are not beggars knocking on the kitchen door; we are heirs entering the throne room with covenant papers in hand. Here is a **Kingdom lexicon** to

enlarge how you approach God:

> *Let me tell you what God said next. He said, "You're my son, And today is your birthday. 8 What do you want? Name it: Nations as a present? continents as a prize? 9 You can command them all to dance for you, Or throw them out with tomorrow's trash." 10 So, rebel-kings, use your heads;Upstart-judges, learn your lesson:*
> Psalm 2:7-10 MSG

- **Decree** – A royal pronouncement aligned with the written will of the King (Job 22:28). Decrees **establish** realities on earth already ratified in Heaven.
- **Petition** – A formal request (1 Samuel 1:17) citing **statute** (Scripture), **precedent** (testimony), and **jurisdiction** (Christ's authority).
- **Summons** – A call to resources and people assigned to your mandate to appear and serve (Isaiah 60:4–11).
- **Injunction** – A binding order restraining demonic interference or unlawful opposition (Matthew 18:18).
- **Writ of Repossession** – A demand for the

return of stolen goods, time, territory, or opportunities (Joel 2:25).

- **Quiet Title Action** – Prayer to clear competing claims on land, assignments, or relationships, establishing **clean title** under Christ's Lordship (Psalm 24:1).
- **Power of Attorney** – Acting in Jesus' name (John 14:13–14; 16:23) as His authorized representative.
- **Territorial Claim** – A documented, prayed-through assertion of inheritance over places, markets, and domains (Joshua 1:3).

When Psalm 2:7–10 says, *"I will declare the decree: The Lord has said to Me, 'You are My Son, Today I have begotten You. Ask of Me, and I will give You the nations for Your inheritance, And the ends of the earth for Your possession. You shall break them with a rod of iron; You shall dash them to pieces like a potter's vessel.' Now therefore, be wise, O kings; Be instructed, you judges of the earth"* (NKJV), God is not inviting us to think small. He is retraining our spiritual vocabulary. Royal sons and daughters must pray in the language of kings, not beggars. Our petitions must match His throne, not our limitations. To walk in this dimension, we must overhaul our prayer vocabulary.

1. Stop Asking for Crumbs - Start Requesting Continents

Most believers still pray as though God's pantry is running out. We whisper for "just enough" when He has already authorized us to inherit entire nations. When the King says, *"Ask Me for the nations"*, it's not poetry, it's an open-ended legal decree. In the courts of Heaven, the scale of your request is evidence of your faith. Small prayers reveal a small view of God.

When you begin praying for entire regions, industries, and spheres of influence, you shift from survival mode to dominion mode. A royal son does not stand at the edge of the table hoping for scraps; he sits at the table and calls for the main course. God is not intimidated by your biggest request, He's insulted by your smallest. When your vision expands, your words will follow.

Jesus never said, "Pray to survive until next week." He said, *"Your kingdom come. Your will be done on earth as it is in heaven"* (Matthew 6:10, NKJV). That's not a crumb prayer, that's a continental prayer. Heaven doesn't ration; Heaven overflows. Your prayer life must match Heaven's scale.

2. Replace Begging with Decreeing

Begging is the language of orphans; decreeing is the language of heirs. A decree is a king's legal pronouncement that changes reality. *"You will also declare a thing, And it will be established for you; So light will shine on your ways"* (Job 22:28, NKJV). This is not wishful thinking, it is the legal exercise of spiritual authority.

When you decree, you are not trying to persuade God to act, you are enforcing what He has already willed. This is why Jesus could say to the fig tree, *"Let no one eat fruit from you ever again."* And His disciples heard it (Mark 11:14, NKJV), and it obeyed without question. Decreeing is not passive; it is legislative. You are Heaven's parliament on earth, passing binding laws in the spirit that creation must obey.

Decreeing shifts your inner posture. Instead of approaching God with a tone of desperation, you speak with the tone of possession. The moment you shift from "Lord, please" to "In the name of Jesus, it shall be so", the atmosphere bends to your voice. This is why royal prayer is not timid, it is commanding.

3. Upgrade "Daily Bread" to "Global Dominion"

The "daily bread" prayer in *"Give us this day our daily bread"* (Matthew 6:11, NKJV) is not an invitation to limit your requests, it is a foundation. Bread is basic; dominion is destiny. Royal prayer builds upon the basics and reaches for the highest purposes of God. *"He shall have dominion also from sea to sea, And from the River to the ends of the earth"* (Psalm 72:8, NKJV). That is the scale of prayer a son should pray.

When you pray for dominion, you are not praying for selfish expansion, you are aligning yourself with God's eternal plan to fill the earth with His glory. This is the prayer Elijah prayed when he called down fire on Mount Carmel: *"Lord God of Abraham, Isaac, and Israel, let it be known this day that You are God in Israel and I am Your servant, and that I have done all these things at Your word. Hear me, O Lord, hear me, that this people may know that You are the Lord God, and that You have turned their hearts back to You again"* (1 Kings 18:36-37, NKJV). He wasn't asking for dinner, he was asking for a divine display that would turn the hearts of an entire nation.

The Church has often mistaken humility for playing small. But kingdom humility is not shrinking, it's submitting your massive vision to God's massive will. You were not saved to stay local in your thinking; you were saved to think global in your praying.

4. Stop Talking in Probabilities - Start Speaking in Certainties

The vocabulary of probability is filled with words like "maybe," "hopefully," and "if it's possible." These phrases have no place in the mouth of a royal heir who knows the will of the King. *"Now this is the confidence that we have in*

Him, that if we ask anything according to His will, He hears us. And if we know that He hears us, whatever we ask, we know that we have the petitions that we have asked of Him" (1 John 5:14–15, NKJV). Royal prayer speaks with the confidence of ownership, not the uncertainty of gambling.

When Jesus spoke to the storm in Mark 4:39, He didn't say, "Storm, if it's alright, could you calm down?" *"Then He arose and rebuked the wind, and said to the sea, 'Peace, be still!' And the wind ceased and there was a great calm"* (Mark 4:39, NKJV). Certainty in prayer is not arrogance, it's alignment with divine order. It's the difference between a servant timidly suggesting and a king issuing a decree.

Your prayer life will never rise above your certainty. If you keep inserting "ifs" into your petitions, you're undermining your own authority. Royal sons pray in the language of inevitability: "This will happen." When Heaven hears that tone, the angels move faster, because they recognize it as the dialect of the throne.

5. Exchange "Survival Prayers" for "History-Making Declarations"

Survival prayers keep you afloat; history-making declarations change the course of nations. In Acts 4:29–31, the early church didn't pray for safety after being threatened, they prayed: *"Now, Lord, look on their threats, and grant to Your servants that with all boldness they may speak Your word, by stretching out Your hand to heal, and that signs and wonders may be done through the name of Your holy Servant Jesus."* And when they had prayed, *"the place where they were assembled together was shaken; and they were all filled with the Holy Spirit, and they spoke the word of God with boldness"* (NKJV). The result? The place shook, and they went on to alter the spiritual climate of entire regions.

History is shaped by those who dare to pray audaciously. Joshua's prayer in Joshua 10:12-14 records:

> *"Then Joshua spoke to the Lord in the day when the Lord delivered up the Amorites before the children of Israel, and he said in the sight of Israel: 'Sun, stand still over Gibeon; And Moon, in the Valley of Aijalon.' So the sun stood still, And the moon stopped, Till the people had revenge upon their enemies… And there has been no day like that, before it or after it, that the Lord heeded the voice of a man; for the Lord fought for Israel"* (NKJV).

That wasn't just about winning a battle; it was about rewriting the rules of creation to accomplish God's purpose. That is what royal prayer does, it bends time, space, and circumstance to align with Heaven's assignment.

If your prayers are small enough to be accomplished without God, you're not yet praying royally. Royal prayer demands miracles. It forces the unseen to manifest. It dares to say, "Lord, make history through me." The size of your prayer determines the size of your legacy.

Pray scripture like legal code, prophesy like government, worship like coronation, and then plan like a builder with permits in hand.

Psalm 2 for Believing Sons: From Theology to Tactics
Identity: "Thou art my Son." In Christ you are not merely tolerated, you are named. Identity precedes authority. The timid cannot steward nations; sons can.
Timing: "This day have I begotten thee." The decree is **present tense.** Do not postpone your boldness to "one day." Heaven's calendar reads **today**.
Scope: "Ask of me… the uttermost parts of the earth." If your ask can be achieved by hustle alone, it is too small. Psalm 2 sets the floor of request at **continental.**
Mechanism: "I will declare the decree." Declare what God has decreed. Faith echoes. The King's court expects agreement, not improvisation.
Outcome: "Thou shalt break… thou shalt dash." God's offer includes both **possession** and **power** to dismantle systems that resist righteous rule. This is not permission to bully; it

is permission to **govern**; to topple what crushes people and erect what blesses them.

Tactically, Psalm 2 means you can pray **macro**: for legal systems to align with justice, for energy grids to stabilize, for supply chains to favor the righteous, for awakening to break like morning across nations. It means you can ask for **land, licenses, labs, libraries, legislative seats, lighthouses**; every gate through which culture is steered.

The Size of God's Offer
God measures gifts in **nations and generations**. He gave Abraham the **land** and the **world** (Genesis 13:14–17; Romans 4:13). He gave Joseph **storehouses** and an **empire's logistics** (Genesis 41). He gave Solomon **wisdom and wealth** that attracted rulers (1 Kings 10). He offered His Son **every kingdom** (rightly, from the Father; falsely, from the tempter). God does not traffic in trinkets. When He says, "Ask," He imagines **city-shaping schools, continent-spanning companies, justice-reforming coalitions, disease-ending innovations, landed legacies** that outlive you by centuries.

So enlarge the frame: ask for a **coastline**, not just a cottage; a **sector**, not just a salary; a **network**, not just a nod. If that sounds grandiose, remember: humility is not asking **less** than God offered; humility is agreeing with His offer and giving Him the glory when it arrives.

Five Audacious, History-Bending Prayers (and How to Pray Like Them)

The Bible is a treasury of impossible asks. Here are **five daring, precedent-setting prayers** (beyond Joshua's long day) that teach sons and daughters how to ask at Psalm-2 scale.

1) Hezekiah's Backward Shadow - Time Reversed at a King's Word

Text: 2 Kings 20:1–11; Isaiah 38:7–8

What happened: Hezekiah, terminally ill, pleads for more years. God grants fifteen years to his life and to **seal the word,** the shadow on Ahaz's sundial goes **back ten degrees.** Time's arrow bends.

Why it's audacious: Hezekiah does not negotiate for comfort; he requests **years** and **a cosmic sign.** He asks for **time itself** to witness the covenant.

How to pray like this:
- Redeem the clock: "Father, reverse the losses of wasted years; compress processes; accelerate approvals; slow what should not rush." (Joel 2:25)
- Ask for seals: Request **undeniable confirmations,** not to satisfy unbelief, but to strengthen

stakeholders and silence accusers.
- Govern deadlines: Lay before God the contracts, court dates, and funding windows; ask for **divine rescheduling.**

2) Elijah's fire and flood - Heaven Answers By Elements

Text: 1 Kings 18:36–39; 1 Kings 17:1; James 5:17–18

What happened: Elijah prays; fire falls on water-drenched sacrifice; a nation turns. He prays again; **drought breaks.**

Why it's audacious: He asks for **public, atmospheric signs** that topple an idolatrous regime in one day. This is not private comfort, it is **national course-correction.**

How to pray like this:
- Target altars: "Answer by fire" where false narratives rule: campuses, newsrooms, courts - so hearts bow to truth.
- Legislate weather in crisis: In famine or flood, pray like James dares us: effectual, fervent decrees that bless life and reveal the Father's kindness.
- Expect civic joy: Pray not only for rain but for the re-evangelization of a region after the rain.

3) Moses at the Sea - Geography Edits Itself

Text: Exodus 14:13–31

What happened: God tells Moses to stretch his hand; the

sea stands up; Israel crosses; the same waters collapse on oppression.

Why it's audacious: Moses doesn't ask for a raft, he commands an ocean. Deliverance arrives as infrastructure: a road through water.

How to pray like this:
- Refuse false options: When culture says "retreat or drown," **ask for the third way** no one sees yet.
- Pray dual outcomes: "Path for the righteous; prison for oppression." Let the **same event** free many and end predation.
- Stretch what's in your hand: Use existing authority, assets, and skill, then expect creation to **cooperate.**

4) Samuel's Thunder-Day - Weather Becomes a Witness
Text: 1 Samuel 12:16–18
What happened: During harvest **(when thunder is rare)**, Samuel calls for storm; God thunders; the people tremble and repent.
Why it's audacious: He asks for **impossible timing,** a sign precisely **when** it should not happen, to validate the word.
How to pray like this:
- Request improbable providences: Not parlor tricks, but **pastorally** targeted signs that humble the

proud and heal the teachable.
- Tie signs to teaching: Samuel explains the sign's meaning; pray for **didactic wonders** that interpret themselves.
- Guard against spectacle: Aim always for **repentance, justice, and joy,** not applause.

5) The Praying Church and Opened Prisons - Systems Let Go

Texts: Acts 12:5–11; Acts 16:25–26; Acts 4:29–31

What happened: The church prays; Peter walks past iron gates under angelic escort. Paul and Silas sing; an earthquake opens cells; captors become converts. After a corporate prayer, **the place is shaken,** and boldness fills the saints.

Why it's audacious: They ask for **state-level intervention:** carceral systems to yield; not one man's comfort only, but **missional continuity**.

How to pray like this:
- Name the gate: Court rulings, regulatory barriers, visas, embargoes; command gates to **open** for the gospel.
- Sing before shaking: Worship is often the lever that turns stone to sand.
- Ask for boldness, not escape: The answer to pres-

sure is power. Pray for **tongues of steel**, not safer rooms.

How To Ask Big Every Day

1) **Begin with the decree:** Read Psalm 2 aloud. Insert the names of your city, sector, and mandate: "Father, as Your son/daughter in the Son, I ask for [**Nations/Markets/Regions**] as inheritance, [**Specific Ends of the Earth**] as possession."

2) **Enlarge the canvas:** Before you ask for a door, ask for the **building**; before the building, ask for **zoning**; before zoning, ask for **favor in city hall**. Pray the **stack**, not the slice.

3) **Trade motives:** Psalm 2 kings kiss the Son, not their brand. Purify ambition. Ask to **bless, build, heal, educate, employ, disciple.**

4) **Specify outcomes:** Name salaries lifted, laws amended, pollutants reduced, clinics opened, languages reached, patents granted, acreage acquired, interest rates favorably negotiated.

5) **Set review dates:** Put **checkpoints** on the calendar. Royal petitions have timelines. Return with thanksgiving for partials and leverage them as **precedent** for finals.

6) **Pair prayer with plan:** Write the budget, org

chart, Gantt, risk register. Psalm 2 heirs **engineer their asks.**

7) Build alliances: Share the decree with intercessors, financiers, technologists, lawmakers. **Distributed agreement** multiplies manifestation.

Prayers, Decrees, and Language for Heirs
Royal Decree (Psalm 2 Frame)

> "Father of our Lord Jesus Christ, who has seated Him above all rule and has seated us with Him, I declare Your decree: You said, 'You are my Son; this day I have begotten You.' Therefore I ask, grant [**name the nation/sector/region**] as inheritance and [**define the ends of the earth relevant to your call**] as possession. Assign angels to open the gates; restrain rulers who war against righteousness; enthrone justice in [**courts/agencies/boards**]; release wealth flows to fund [**schools/clinics/labs/factories/churches**]. Let the kings be wise and the judges instructed by Your fear. In Jesus' name. Amen."

Writ of Repossession (Joel 2 Frame)

> "In the name of Jesus, I demand the return of

stolen time, contracts, customers, creativity, and courage. I invoke Heaven's restitution policy: 'I will restore the years…' I command the devourer to disgorge what he has eaten. I declare back-pay, back-rent, back-interest, and back-honor, with interest and costs, returned sevenfold (Proverbs 6:31)."

Injunction Against Interference (Matthew 18 Frame)

"I bind every spirit and scheme that frustrates **permits, partnerships, payrolls, and production.** I loose favor with inspectors, bankers, neighbors, and networks. I forbid sabotage; I permit synergy. What I bind and loose here is bound and loosed in Heaven's court."

Territorial Claim (Joshua 1 Frame)

"Every place the sole of my foot treads in [**address/coordinates/market**] is given to me to steward. I plant the banner of Christ in **this** ground. Let the land yield its strength; let the people flourish; let righteousness and peace kiss in this place."

Obstacles to Big Asking (and How Sons Overcome)
- **Religious smallness:** A culture that confuses restraint with holiness. Cure it by **meditating on big promises** until your insides match God's outside.
- **Trauma from delay:** Disappointments that shrank your expectations. Cure it by **testimony therapy.** Feast on God's track record, not on your timeline.
- **Guilt about gain:** Conflate wealth with worldliness. Cure it by embracing **custodianship.** Resources in righteous hands heal nations.
- **Fear of man:** Worry about optics. Cure it by remembering **audacity honors the Offerer** when it's aimed at blessing.

Let's translate the royal frame into two real-world domains, land and innovation, so you can see the mechanics.

Land acquisition (Psalm-2 style)
1. **Pray the perimeter (walk, drive, map):** read Psalm 2; claim boundaries; record impressions.
2. **File in two courts:** submit zoning/permit paperwork; submit decrees to Heaven daily.
3. **Name the purpose:** schools, housing, clinics, farms. God funds function, not vanity.
4. **Assemble the stack:** intercessors + civil engineers + financiers + neighbors + council advocates.

5. **Ask big:** go beyond parcel to corridor, beyond corridor to district impact.
6. **Install an altar:** monthly worship/thanksgiving on site.
7. **Tell the story:** raise faith by reporting each win; each becomes **precedent** for the next parcel.

Innovation pipeline (Psalm-2 style)
1. **Problem selection:** pick a pain large enough to justify nations as the scope (energy, water, housing, literacy, disease).
2. **Prayer sprints:** 21–40 days of decrees for **ideas, team, data, design.**
3. **Prototype quickly:** faith does not fear iteration; it **accelerates** it.
4. **Protect and publish:** IP strategy + open-access generosity where it multiplies impact.
5. **Policy bridge:** influence regulations so adoption scales ethically.
6. **Patient capital:** recruit Kingdom investors who value **impact + sustainability**, not hype.
7. **Tithing to the future:** dedicate a portion of profits to training the next generation who will steward the tech.

A Birthday Benediction - Now Ask

Today is your royal birthday in Christ. The Father has not laid a cupcake with a candle before you; He has rolled out a **continent** with cities still unnamed. He has set **oceans** whose currents can feed the poor and power the lights. He has placed **languages** still waiting for songs, **laws** still waiting for justice, **lands** still waiting for heirs. And over it all He has said one operative word: **"Ask."**

So ask like a son: for nations to be discipled, for universities to be reborn, for ports to be cleared of corruption, for rivers to run clean, for forests to be stewarded, for grids to be resilient, for clinics to cure what fear says is incurable, for courts to love truth, for cities to dance again. Ask for the **uttermost parts** and then plan, build, hire, design, legislate, teach, and serve until your prayer wears boots.

> "Father, this day we declare Your decree. In Christ we are Your sons and daughters. We ask You for nations as inheritance and the ends of the earth as possession. Make our motives pure, our plans excellent, our courage durable, our love unmistakable. Let our audacious requests become public testimonies that You are exactly as generous as Psalm 2 says You are. Amen."

Chapter 15

☙

Faith: The Greatest Activator of the Power of God

Faith is the key that opens every door in the Kingdom of God. It is the master activator of divine power, the currency of Heaven, and the force that transforms invisible promises into tangible realities. Without faith, the Scriptures declare, *"it is impossible to please God"* (Hebrews 11:6, NKJV), but *"with faith, nothing is impossible"* (Mark 9:23). Faith is not passive belief. Rather it is aggressive trust, confident expectation, and bold action upon God's word.

Throughout the Bible, God makes staggering promises to those who believe.

The **first promise** is that faith brings the impossible within reach. Jesus said to the desperate father, *"If you can believe, all things are possible to him who believes"* (Mark 9:23, NKJV). The scope here is limitless: all things. Faith eliminates the category of "impossible." It is the power that moves mountains (Mark 11:23) and commands storms to be still. This is not fantasy; it is the operation of spiritual law. When faith is active, you have legal access to every miracle Heaven can provide.

The **second promise** is that faith unlocks the rewards of God. Hebrews 11:6 continues, *"...for he who comes to God must believe that He is, and that He is a rewarder of those who diligently seek Him"* (NKJV). Faith is not just believing in God's existence, it is believing in His generosity. A faith-filled person expects divine reward and lives as though the reward is already on the way. This expectation itself pulls the future into the present.

The **third promise** is that faith gives you victory over the world. "For whatever is born of God overcomes the world. And this is the victory that has overcome the world—our faith" (1 John 5:4, NKJV). Faith is the believer's victory mechanism. It overrides the limitations of economics, culture, politics, and even biology. A world-conquering believer is not a product of ideal circumstances. They are a product of unshakable confidence in God's word.

The **fourth promise** is that faith grants access to divine power. Paul writes, "Therefore, having been justified by faith, we have peace with God through our Lord Jesus

Christ, through whom also we have access by faith into this grace in which we stand…" (Romans 5:1-2, NKJV). Grace is God's supernatural ability; His operational power in your life and faith is the key that opens its vault. You do not stumble into grace; you step into it through faith.

The **fifth promise** is that faith transfers the blessing of Abraham to you. "So then those who are of faith are blessed with believing Abraham" (Galatians 3:9, NKJV). The same covenant that made Abraham wealthy, influential, and globally significant now rests on the shoulders of every believer who walks by faith. This is not a religious metaphor, it is a legal inheritance.

Abraham's life is the masterclass on how faith changes history. God told him, *"I will make you a great nation; I will bless you and make your name great; and you shall be a blessing… and in you all the families of the earth shall be blessed"* (Genesis 12:2-3, NKJV). He believed God without a roadmap. He left his homeland, wandered through territories that did not yet belong to him, and lived as a stranger while holding title deeds in Heaven. Hebrews 11:8-10 tells us that he lived "by faith" in tents while looking for a city whose builder and maker is God.

Abraham's faith did more than secure his personal blessing. It gave birth to nations. His two sons, Ishmael and Isaac, became fathers of dynasties. Today, the descendants of both lines possess some of the greatest concentrations of wealth on earth. The Arab nations, largely from Ishmael's lineage, control vast oil reserves. The Jewish people, from Isaac's line, dominate sectors of global finance, innovation, and technology.

Paul declares in Ephesians 2:12–13 that once we were *"...aliens from the commonwealth of Israel and strangers from the covenants of promise, having no hope and without God in the world. But now in Christ Jesus you who once were far off have been brought near by the blood of Christ"* (NKJV). Through Christ, every believer gains full citizenship in this commonwealth; a spiritual and material inheritance secured by covenant. The same blessing that fueled Abraham's prosperity, guided Joseph's rise, empowered David's reign, and multiplied Solomon's wealth now belongs to us. We are no longer strangers; we are rightful heirs.

The patriarchs were not poor shepherds eking out a living. They were multi-generational billionaires in today's terms. Abraham's fortune (estimated modern value: **$10–$15 billion**) included silver, gold, herds, flocks, and servants (Genesis 13:2). His wealth multiplied through divine guidance, strategic alliances (like with Mamre, Eshcol, and Aner), and covenant promises. Isaac (estimated worth: **$12–$14 billion**) practiced contrarian investing, sowing in famine and reaping a hundredfold (Genesis 26:12–14). His agricultural innovation and livestock management made him "very wealthy." Jacob (estimated worth: **$8–$10 billion**) mastered bioengineering in animal husbandry (Genesis 30:37–43). Through selective breeding and divine insight, he built a livestock empire. Joseph (estimated worth: **$15–$20 billion**) used crisis economics during Egypt's famine to centralize resources under Pharaoh, managing a global grain monopoly (Genesis 41). David (estimated worth: **$40 billion**) amassed wealth through military conquest, tribute from subdued nations, and trade networks. Solomon (estimated worth: **$2.2 trillion**) leveraged wisdom to create global trade routes, maritime ventures, and high-value imports of gold, silver, and exotic goods (1 Kings 10:21–23).

These men operated by revelation, strategy, and faith, building empires that shaped the world's economy. Their wealth was not accidental, it was covenant-driven, strategically managed, and spiritually sustained. And because of Christ, the same faith that empowered them is now alive in us, calling us to rise as innovators, entrepreneurs, pioneers, and world-changers.

Marketplace Dominance By Faith
Let us now construct a strategy, by faith, to create marketplace dominance by doing a practical deep dive that shows

how covenant blessing and biblical innovation, and wealth patterns translate into **territorial ownership, market dominance, and global influence** for believers **today**. It is grounded, strategic, and immediately usable while staying faithful to the faith-first mandate of Scripture.

ଙ

Understand Dominion Economics: How Covenant Wealth Becomes Land, Markets, and Global Reach

Dominion Economics requires we understand the covenant, how to translate faith to assets, prioritize landownership, dominate the market, innovate mercilessly, finance, and gatekeep. We must build with succession in mind, exercise righteous compliance, plan the launch, measure performance and visualize the grand model. We must formulate our prayers and decrees, guard our hearts, and move from blessing to blueprint. It is a formidable assignment with many moving parts. Yet we are each fearfully and wonderfully made, making up the Body who is equipped to work collectively to enact the covenant that still extends to God's people.

Let's break it apart into actionable steps for acute understanding.

1) Know The Covenant: Why Believers Can and Must Build at Scale

The first and most important part of dominion economics is knowing this:

The permission is already signed.

Scripture says, *"So then those who are of faith are blessed with believing Abraham"* (Galatians 3:9, NKJV). *"The earth is the Lord's, and all its fullness"* (Psalm 24:1). *"Ask of Me, and I will give You the nations for Your inheritance"* (Psalm 2:8). In Christ, we were *"no longer strangers… but fellow citizens"* in the **commonwealth of Israel** (Ephesians 2:12–13). That word **commonwealth** is economic. It means shared resources, laws, rights, and responsibilities. Covenant blessing is not a private feeling; it's a legal **framework** that authorizes believers to create, own, and govern tangible assets for multi-generational Kingdom purposes.

Anchor conviction: We have been given dominion. Dominion is stewardship, not domination. We build to **bless:** to heal systems, employ people, educate children, clean water, stabilize power, reform justice, and distribute the fruits of wisdom (Isaiah 58; Jeremiah 29:7; Matthew 5:14–16).

2) Translate Faith to Assets: The "Abraham-to-Assets" Pipeline

Faith becomes influence when it becomes assets. The patriarchs converted revelation into land, herds, trade routes, and treasuries. Here's a modernized pipeline:

1. Revelation → Mandate
Seek God for a clear sphere (land, housing, energy, food, health, education, media, finance, logistics). Write a one-sentence mandate: "We exist to _____ for _____ by _____."

2. Mandate → Territory
Define the **where**: a neighborhood, city, corridor, or digital market. Prayer-walk it. Study its laws, needs, and choke points. Claim it in prayer and planning.

3. Territory → Vehicle
Choose the **legal and economic** vehicle (trusts, LLCs, co-ops, foundations, funds, public-private partnerships). Covenant wealth travels on rails.

4. Vehicle → Assets
Acquire **land** (priority), then infrastructure (water, power, warehousing), then productive assets (farms, factories, clinics, schools), then intellectual property (patents, curricula, software).

5. Assets → Cashflows

Design resilient revenue: long leases, diversified customers, recurring service contracts, export channels, and royalty-bearing IP.

6. Cashflows → Multipliers

Reinvest in R&D, workforce upskilling, vertical integration, and new territories. Tithe as strategy: fund the very ecosystems (churches, schools, clinics) that stabilize your market.

7. Multipliers → Generations

Succession, trusts, governance charters, leadership pipelines. Bless **children's children** (Proverbs 13:22).

3) Land First: The Patriarchal Priority

Abraham, Isaac, and Jacob anchored wealth in land because land is the platform of all other productivity.

Action plan (12–24 months):

- **Discern & Delineate:** Identify a target zone (e.g., 500–5,000 acres rural; 5–50 acres urban infill; an industrial estate; a coastal logistics node). Map utilities, zoning, transit, flood lines, and policy roadmaps.
- **Assemble Quietly:** Secure options, rights of first refusal, and phased closings; engage

community early with a benefit plan (jobs, training, services, green space).
- **Bless the Soil:** Prayer-walk, dedicate, and decree Psalm 24 and Deuteronomy 28 over the land. Then **test the soil** (literal: agronomy; figurative: stakeholder sentiment).
- **Develop in Rings:** Core (anchor users: school, clinic, hub church, food market), Middle (housing/SMEs), Outer (logistics, light manufacturing, agritech). The altar (worship & justice) is **central**, not peripheral.

Why land? It compounds quietly, collateralizes growth, and outlives fads. It is also where you can visibly heal creation through soil regeneration, water stewardship, tree canopy, biodiversity; turning dominion into **shalom**.

4) Market Dominance: Joseph's Crisis Playbook

Joseph did four things: foreknowledge, storage, logistics, and policy (Genesis 41). Modern read:

- **Data & Foresight:** Build dashboards on the "seven lean years" of your sector (supply risk, regulatory shifts, demographic waves). Pray for dreams; hire data scientists.
- **Storage & Buffering:** Create buffers like in-

ventory, cash, credit lines, strategic reserves (grain then; energy, chips, medicine now).
- **Logistics & Distribution:** Control the **last mile.** Own warehouses, fleets, and software that allocate scarcity fairly but profitably.
- **Policy Interface:** Counsel "Pharaoh." Participate in standards, safety codes, energy policy, health guidelines so good governance scales your impact.

Dominance in the Kingdom is service at scale. You win markets because you **carry** people through crisis reliably, ethically, repeatedly.

5) Innovation as Covenant Craft: Jacob's "Bioengineering" Mindset

Jacob didn't cheat Laban; he out-innovated him (Genesis 30:37–43). He observed traits, designed pairings, and built a **resilient genotype portfolio;** a premodern IP strategy.

Modern parallels:
- **Agritech:** Soil microbes, drought-tolerant crops, regenerative grazing.
- **Biotech/Medtech:** Low-cost diagnostics, cold-chain-lite vaccines, AI triage.
- **CivTech:** Grid micro-islands, water reclamation, modular housing, disaster-resilient

design.
- **FinTech:** Transparent microcredit, value-stable settlement rails for SMEs.
- **EdTech:** Bilingual literacy platforms, skilled-trades simulators, AI tutors for underserved learners.

Playbook:
(1) Pray for insight → (2) Rapid prototype → (3) Protect IP wisely → (4) Ethical trials with real users → (5) Scale with mission-aligned capital → (6) Train local operators → (7) Share blueprints where it multiplies justice.

6) Finance: Solomon's Port-to-Palace System
Solomon knit **ports, fleets, trade treaties, and knowledge networks** (1 Kings 10). You can, too.

- **Four Capitals: Financial** (money), **Social** (trust), **Intellectual** (know-how), **Spiritual** (favor). Track and grow all four.
- **Capital Stack:** Grants/Donor-advised funds (public good), patient equity (long horizon), senior debt (asset-backed), revenue share (mission fit).
- **Risk Shields:** Multi-entity structure, reserves policy, key-person plans, compliance hygiene, and covenantal ethics (no bribery/

exploitation).

- **Cashflow Creed:** "Own boring, cash-rich assets" (utilities, warehousing, rentals) plus "build category-creating IP" (higher upside, global reach).

Tithe & Alms as Strategy: Fund justice **where you operate**. This includes legal aid, nutrition, schools. It lowers crime, boosts talent, and cements social license to operate.

7) Gatekeeping: Daniel's Court Craft

Dominion requires **gate access** to regulators, mayors, ministers, editors, educators. Daniel didn't abandon prayer to gain the palace; he used prayer **to serve** the palace (Daniel 1, 6).

Gatekeeping in Practice:

- **Adopt a city gate** (zoning board, school board, port authority, health commission).
- **Offer pro-bono** research and draft solutions.
- **Be unfailingly ethical. Excellence earns hearing; integrity sustains it.**
- Teach your team the "court protocol" of clarity, brevity, numbers, and humility.

8) People Power: Bezalel's Guilds and Succession

Bezalel was **Spirit-filled** to design and craft (Exodus 31:1–5). Excellence is an anointing, not just a work ethic.

Build the guild:
- Apprenticeships for teens, paid fellowships for grads, residencies for mid-career switchers.
- A "Solomon School" for procurement, trade, and cross-border compliance.
- Leadership lattice (not just ladder): rotate leaders through land, finance, operations, and community engagement to grow **rounded stewards**.

Succession: Put it in writing. Custodian boards, mission locks, buy-sell agreements, trusts with values clauses. Dominion fades without succession.

9) Righteous Compliance: Holiness as Competitive Advantage

Holiness isn't a handicap; it's **risk management and brand moat**.

- **No corruption.** Refuse kickbacks and predatory terms. You'll lose some deals and gain the ones that matter.
- **Transparent accounting.** Clean books in-

vite clean partners.
- **Worker dignity.** Living wages, safety, skill ladders, family leave. Loyalty is priceless.
- Environmental stewardship. Regenerate what you use. Creation cooperates with those who bless it.

10) Twelve-Month Launch Blueprint

Q1: Foundation - Mandate, territory, legal entities, prayer network, feasibility, seed budget.

Q2: Land & Alliances - Site control/LOIs, stakeholder compacts, initial permitting, anchor tenant/partner MOUs.

Q3: Finance & Build - Capital stack closed, phase-1 infrastructure, first hires, community benefits roll-out.

Q4: Operate & Signal - Soft launch core services, publish outcomes, certify standards, pipeline phase-2/3.

Weekly rhythm: Word & worship (identity), intercession & decrees (authority), dashboards & stand-ups (execution), testimonies (culture).

11) Key Performance Indicators for Kingdom Builders
Also known as **KPI,** these are worship metrics when they measure how love becomes structure. KPI's are means to measure and evaluate the success of a business, organization, or an employee. KPI's can be:

- **Land:** acreage controlled; % entitled; soil/water indices improving.
- **Jobs:** # created; median wage vs. local median; training hours.
- **Households:** housing units delivered; utility reliability; clinic throughput; school seats.
- **Finance:** DSCR, reserves months, revenue diversity, R&D intensity.
- **Justice:** contracts to local SMEs; legal outcomes; carbon/waste reductions.
- **Discipleship:** baptisms, groups, volunteer hours, youth apprentices.

12) Prayer–Decree Toolkit (Use Daily, Then Build)
- **Inheritance Decree** (Psalm 2/ Ephesians 2): "Father, in Christ I am no longer a stranger but a citizen of the commonwealth. I ask for **[territory/sector]** as inheritance and decree the ends of **[region/market]** as possession. Seat favor on our plans; scatter resistance that

harms people; enthrone justice in the gates."
- **Land Title Decree** (Joshua 1/Psalm 24):
"This land is the Lord's. I claim clean title under Jesus' name. Every prior claim rooted in injustice is resolved by restitution and mercy. Let the soil yield its strength and the people flourish."
- **Joseph Provision Decree** (Genesis 41 / Psalm 105):
"Give foresight, strategy, storage, and favor. Make us a refuge in crisis and a witness of Your goodness."
- **Solomon Wisdom Decree** (1 Kings 3):
"Grant understanding hearts to govern people and projects. Add what we did not ask because we asked for what You value."

Then put steel under those words: budgets, contracts, schedules, and teams.

13) Create the Model: What This Looks Like on the Ground

A. The Kingdom District (Urban Infill, 7–10 Years)

Acquire a blighted corridor. Phase in: (1) mixed-income housing + hub church + health clinic; (2) vocational academy (trades, nursing, coding); (3) SME market hall; (4) solar micro-grid + water reuse; (5) justice center (legal aid, family services). Finance with blended capital; lock rent affordability; measure crime drop, wage rise, school outcomes. Spin off a neighborhood REIT with mission guardrails for citizen ownership.

B. *The Joseph Valley (Rural 3–5K Acres, 10–15 Years)*
Aggregate farms; deploy regen agriculture, grain storage, cold chain, and a food processing park. Add a K–12/tech campus, telehealth node, and intermodal logistics spur. Export branded high-integrity foods. Create a farmer co-op with profit share. Track soil carbon, water tables, and household incomes. Train 1,000 youth into ag-tech, mechanics, and coding tied to local industry.

Both are **cathedrals of usefulness;** altars made of schools, clinics, warehouses, and orchards.

14) Guard the Heart: Faith + Love + Holiness
- **Faith** activates the power (Mark 9:23).
- **Love** governs the power (1 Corinthians 13).
- **Holiness** protects the power (John 14:30).

Power without love becomes predatory; love without power becomes sentimental; power without holiness leaks. Keep all three and you'll **carry** what you build.

15) Final Charge: From Blessing to Blueprint
Abraham believed and pitched tents on promises that later became nations. Jacob innovated, turning knowledge into

herds. Joseph governed; turning famine into a logistics empire. David secured, turning victories into stable borders. Solomon connected, turning wisdom into global trade.

Now it's our turn. In Christ, we are heirs of the **commonwealth** and carriers of the **covenants of promise**. Take the blessing off the page and pour it into **land you can walk, companies you can audit, schools you can visit, patients you can heal, and cities you can bless**. Pray like heirs, plan like builders, partner like family, and persevere like farmers. As you do, the promise to Abraham becomes **public record** in your generation.

> *"So then those who are of faith are blessed with believing Abraham."* (Galatians 3:9)

> *"Ask of Me, and I will give You the nations…"* (Psalm 2:8)

> *"No longer strangers… but fellow citizens."* (Ephesians 2:12–13)

Now…**possess the land, master the markets, and steward the nations for the glory of the King.**

Conclusion

The journey through these pages has been more than an academic or theological exercise. It has been a call to action, a prophetic summons to rise into the fullness of your

God-given mandate. From the moment God said to mankind in Genesis 1:28, "Be fruitful and multiply and fill the earth and subdue it, and have dominion", He set in motion a divine order: His children are to be rulers, managers, and possessors of the earth's resources in alignment with His will.

We have examined the biblical patriarchs, prophets, apostles, and even Christ Himself, all of whom modeled dominion over the material and spiritual realms. We have seen how history records the fierce battles over land, resources, and influence and why the enemy so violently opposes the believer's rise. We have explored the reality of territorial spirits, the laws of the invisible world, and the necessity of mastering them if we are to take possession of what Heaven has promised.

The principle is unshakable: **the earth has been given to the sons of men** (Psalm 115:16). This is not a poetic ideal; it is a transfer of responsibility and authority. God has not called His children to be beggars at the table of the world but to be stewards of its wealth, innovators of its systems, and leaders of its future. Faith, as we have seen, is the ultimate activator of this mandate; faith that does not waver in the face of giants, faith that dares to ask for nations as an inheritance (Psalm 2:8), and faith that turns the unseen into the tangible.

This is not about greed, self-exaltation, or selfish ambition. It is about alignment with Heaven's agenda. The believer's dominion is rooted in God's glory and His desire to fill the earth with the knowledge of Himself. When we occupy land, steward wealth, innovate solutions, and set righteous standards, we extend the borders of His Kingdom.

The time for passive belief has passed. The Kingdom is advancing, and it demands active participation. The call is clear: **own territory, command resources, subdue systems, and manifest the sons of God in every sphere of life.** The whole creation is groaning for it, Heaven is backing it, and history will remember those who answered it.

Now, step forward, not as a tenant in God's world, but as a rightful heir. Your inheritance is vast, your authority is real, and your moment is now. The earth awaits your dominion.

Appendices

Appendix A: Key Scriptures on Dominion and Possessing the Earth

Below is a curated list of biblical passages that form the backbone of this book's message. Each Scripture reveals God's intention for His people to possess, manage, and govern the earth with wisdom and righteousness.

> ***1. Genesis 1:26-28 (ESV)***
>
> *Then God said, "Let us make man in our image, after our likeness. And let them have dominion over the fish of the sea and over the birds of the heavens and over the livestock and over all the earth and over every creeping thing that creeps on the earth." So God created man in his own image, in the image of God he created him; male and female he created them. And God blessed them. And God said to them, "Be fruitful and multiply and fill the earth and sub-*

due it, and have dominion over the fish of the sea and over the birds of the heavens and over every living thing that moves on the earth."

This is humanity's original mandate: a call to mastery, stewardship, and authority over all created things.

2. Deuteronomy 11:24 (ESV)

Every place on which the sole of your foot treads shall be yours. Your territory shall be from the wilderness to the Lebanon and from the River, the river Euphrates, to the western sea.

God's covenant people are given legal right to territory under divine promise.

3. Psalm 2:8 (ESV)

Ask of me, and I will make the nations your heritage, and the ends of the earth your possession.

This is God's invitation for bold, global requests; an open offer for nations and lands.

4. Proverbs 13:22 (ESV)

A good man leaves an inheritance to his children's children, but the sinner's wealth is laid up for the righteous.

A reminder that wealth transfer is inevitable for those aligned with Kingdom purposes.

5. Romans 4:13 (ESV)

For the promise to Abraham and his offspring that he would be heir of the world did not come through the law but through the righteousness of faith.

Faith positions the believer as an heir of the entire world.

Appendix B: Practical Declarations for Dominion

Speak these aloud daily to align your spirit with Heaven's authority:

1. I am made in the image of God; therefore, I carry divine authority over the material world.
2. The earth is the Lord's and the fullness thereof, and as His child, I am an heir to His inheritance.
3. Every place the sole of my foot treads is given to me for the Kingdom.
4. Nations and lands are opening to me by divine appointment.
5. The wealth of the wicked is transferring into my stewardship.
6. My words carry the creative power of God to shift environments and systems.
7. No territorial spirit can resist the authority of Christ in me.

8. I am a master of both the visible and invisible laws of creation.

9. My work, business, and ministry prosper because Heaven backs my assignment.

10. I live to glorify God through my dominion on earth.

Appendix C: Recommended Resources

Books:
- *Anointed for Business* by Ed Silvoso
- *Commanding Your Morning* by Cindy Trimm
- *The Supernatural Power of a Transformed Mind* by Bill Johnson
- *The Wealth Transfer* by Matthew Ashimolowo
- *Releasing Kings for Ministry in the Marketplace* by John Garfield & Harold Eberle

Websites & Study Platforms:
- *Bible Gateway* - Scripture study in multiple translations.
- *Blue Letter Bible* - In-depth word studies and concordance.
- *Quantum Faith by Annette Capps* - A resource on how faith intersects with quantum physics.

Appendix D: Wealth Estimates of Biblical Patriarchs

Patriarch	Estimated Wealth in Today's Value	Source of Wealth
Abraham	$200–$300 billion	Livestock, silver, gold, and land grants from rulers
Isaac	$150 billion	Agriculture, wells, and inherited wealth
Jacob	$100 billion	Livestock breeding (bioengineering via selective mating)
Joseph	$90 billion	Grain monopolies, Pharaoh's economic restructuring
Solomon	$2.2 trillion	International trade, taxation, tribute, gold imports
David	$200 billion	Tribute from nations, military conquests
Job	$50–$70 billion	Livestock, land, and trade

For more information on
Dr. Peter Bonadie

Website:
www.peterbonadieworldwide.org
www.klministries.org

Instagram:
@peterbonadieministries

Facebook:
Facebook.com/drpeterbonadie

www.ingramcontent.com/pod-product-compliance
Lightning Source LLC
Chambersburg PA
CBHW062006180426
43198CB00037B/2475